PENGUIN BOOKS

Understanding Company Financial Statements

R. H. Parker is Emeritus Professor of accounting at the University of Exeter. A graduate of University College London and a fellow of the Institute of Chartered Accountants in England and Wales, he has practised and taught accounting in England, Scotland, France, Nigeria and Australia. He has published many articles and books, including (with C. W. Nobes) *Comparative International Accounting* (ninth edition, 2006). His main research interests are the international, comparative and historical aspects of accounting. He was the British Accounting Association Distinguished Academic of the Year in 1997 and the American Accounting Association's Outstanding International Accounting Educator in 2003. In 1998 he received the Hourglass Award of the Academy of Accounting Historians. He was editor or joint editor of the academic journal *Accounting and Business Research* from 1975 to 1993 and a Professorial Research Fellow of the Institute of Chartered Accountants of Scotland from 1991 to 1996.

Understanding Company Financial Statements

SIXTH EDITION

R. H. Parker

PENGUIN BOOKS

For Theresa and Michael – and Carina

PENGUIN BOOKS

Published by the Penguin Group
Penguin Books Ltd, 80 Strand, London WC2R 0RL, England
Penguin Group (USA) Inc., 375 Hudson Street, New York, New York 10014, USA
Penguin Group (Canada), 90 Eglinton Avenue East, Suite 700, Toronto, Ontario, Canada M4P 2Y3
(a division of Pearson Penguin Canada Inc.)
Penguin Ireland, 25 St Stephen's Green, Dublin 2, Ireland
(a division of Penguin Books Ltd)
Penguin Group (Australia), 250 Camberwell Road, Camberwell, Victoria 3124, Australia
(a division of Pearson Australia Group Pty Ltd)
Penguin Books India Pvt Ltd, 11 Community Centre, Panchsheel Park, New Delhi – 110 017, India
Penguin Group (NZ), 67 Apollo Drive, Rosedale, North Shore 0632, New Zealand
(a division of Pearson New Zealand Ltd)
Penguin Books (South Africa) (Pty) Ltd, 24 Sturdee Avenue, Rosebank, Johannesburg 2196, South Africa

Penguin Books Ltd, Registered Offices: 80 Strand, London WC2R 0RL, England

www.penguin.com

First published 1972
Second Edition 1982
Third Edition 1988
Fourth Edition 1994
Fifth Edition 1999
Sixth Edition 2007
1

Acknowledgements for 'The Hardship of Accounting' from *The Poetry of Robert Frost*, edited by Edward
Connery Lathem: to the estate of Robert Frost, Edward Connery Lathem and to Jonathan Cape Ltd.
Copyright 1936 by Robert Frost. Copyright © 1964 by Lesley Frost Ballantine. Copyright © 1969 by
Holt, Rinehart & Winston, Inc. Reprinted by permission of Holt, Rinehart & Winston, Inc.

Set in 9.5/12 pt PostScript Adobe Minion
Typeset by Rowland Phototypesetting Ltd, Bury St Edmunds, Suffolk
Printed in England by Clays Ltd, St Ives plc

978–0–141–03271–9

Contents

Preface to the Sixth Edition

The eminent company lawyer L. C. B. Gower once wrote of the published financial statements of companies that 'to the average investor or creditor – "the man on the Clapham omnibus" – they are cryptograms which he is incapable of solving'. This small book is an attempt to make the task easier. It is written for the general reader, not for my fellow accountants, and does not pretend to be more than an introduction to a difficult subject. No previous knowledge is assumed. The emphasis is on analysis and interpretation rather than on accounting techniques. Special attention has been paid to making the language of accounting and finance intelligible to the layperson.

This sixth edition retains the general approach of previous editions but the pace of change has been such that much has had to be rewritten. In particular, accounting, auditing and financial reporting in the UK have been increasingly influenced by globalization. From 2005 onwards the consolidated statements of UK listed companies are drawn up in accordance not with UK financial reporting standards but with international financial reporting standards (IFRS). Whilst the book was in preparation, the Companies Act 2006 made its complicated progress towards the statute book. The internet has made access to company financial statements much easier.

There are many references in the book to the published financial statements of real-life UK companies. These are intended as illustrations of common practice, not as positive or negative comments on the companies concerned.

As always, I am greatly indebted to Professor C. W. Nobes for his careful and close reading of the text and for many helpful suggestions.

Christine Down has helped to improve my word processing. Errors and misinterpretations that remain are of course my responsibility.

Companies and Their Reports

In sooth a goodly company.

Revd Richard Harris Barham, 'The Jackdaw of Rheims'

PURPOSE AND DESIGN OF THE BOOK

It is not difficult to obtain a copy of the annual report of a company listed on a UK stock exchange. A hard copy is usually readily available on request from the company, even if the enquirer is not a shareholder. The reports are also available on the company's website and extracts can be downloaded from the internet. There are several annual report services. Much more difficult is understanding the contents of such reports, which are often remarkably voluminous (BP's 2005 report, for example, is 177 pages long). They are not easy reading, even when (as is not always the case) care has been taken in their design and the figures and text are relieved by illustrations. Nevertheless the attempt is worth making, if only because so much of the country's wealth is generated by such companies and so many people depend on them for wages, salaries and pensions.

The purpose of this book is to show the reader how to understand, analyse and interpret these reports, and more especially the financial statements contained therein. In order to do this we shall look in detail at the annual reports of a number of companies. A list of companies referred to and the addresses of their websites are given in Chapter 5.

In this first chapter we survey in general terms the contents of a company annual report and look briefly at the nature and constitution of the limited liability company. Chapter 2 describes the various financial statements and introduces many important financial and accounting concepts and methods. Chapter 3 explains as briefly as possible the nature of company taxation and the functions of auditors. Chapter 4 deals with accounting regulation and, in particular, international financial reporting standards (IFRS). Chapter 5 describes certain tools of analysis and guides the reader towards a multitude of useful websites. Chapter 6 is concerned with profitability and return on investment, Chapter 7 with liquidity and cash flows, and Chapter 8 with sources of funds and capital structure. Chapter 9 summarizes the whole book.

Finance and accounting are specialist subjects. This does not mean that they need remain incomprehensible to the layperson. It does mean, however, that technical terms cannot entirely be avoided. One cannot, after all, learn to drive a car or play a piano without learning some new words. In order to make the learning process as painless as possible, technical terms are explained as they are introduced or shortly thereafter, and a glossary is provided for reference (Appendix B). One unavoidable complication is that British and American terminology differ and that IFRS are written in a mixture of the two. This book uses mainly IFRS terminology but also refers to more traditional British usages where appropriate. It is hoped that some readers will want to know more about finance and accounting. For such readers the websites listed in Chapter 5 and the guide to further reading given in Chapter 9 should be useful.

CONTENTS OF A COMPANY ANNUAL REPORT

No two companies set out their annual reports in exactly the same way, but the following is a fairly common sequence of headings (not always under the exact titles below):

- About the company
- Financial highlights
- Chairman's statement
- Board of directors
- Directors' report*
- Operating and financial review
- Corporate social responsibility review

- Corporate governance*
- Directors' remuneration report*
- Financial statements*
- Auditors' report*
- Five year record
- Shareholder information

One reason for similarities in annual reports is that many items are required by regulation. These have been marked above with an asterisk.

Perhaps the first thing of interest about a company is what it does, which is often not clear from the company's name. Companies give this information under a variety of headings. Unilever (2005 Report) has a five-page 'About Unilever' section elaborating its claim to be 'one of the world's leading suppliers of fast moving consumer goods across foods, home and personal product categories'. Centrica (2005), in a two-page 'Business Overview', lists its main activities as sourcing energy, gas and electricity supply, home services and gas storage.

Most companies provide a 'financial highlights' section and a Chairman's Statement, although these are not legal requirements. The former gives key financial figures such as turnover (sales), operating profit, earnings per share and dividends per share. The content of the latter varies considerably, but typically there is a look both at the immediate past and prospects for the future. Research has shown that this is one of the most widely read sections of an annual report, no doubt because it is usually presented in non-technical language, and because, unlike most of the annual report, it deals with the future as well as the past. Also written in fairly non-technical language are the Operating and Financial Review and the Corporate Social Responsibility Review, which are discussed in later sections of this chapter.

At the head of any company is a Board of Directors. Some companies merely provide a list of its members, but most also provide potted biographies and few can resist photographs. The board of a listed company comprises both executive and non-executive directors, with the positions of chairman and chief executive held in most, but not all, listed companies by different persons. The Directors' Report is a document whose contents, unlike the Chairman's Statement, are largely, but not wholly, determined by legislation. That of British Polythene Industries (BPI) (2005), for example, contains the following headings: principal activity, results, dividends, directors, disabled employees, policy on payment of suppliers, financial risk management, charitable and political donations, auditors, substantial shareholders. Details of the directors' remuneration are given at length in a separate report.

The corporate governance section of an annual report is mainly concerned with the ways in which directors of companies are held accountable to shareholders. This topic is discussed later in this chapter. The auditors' report is discussed in Chapter 3.

The most important section of the annual report (at least from the point of view of this book) is that containing the consolidated financial statements. From the layperson's point of view it is also the most difficult to understand. A 'consolidated' financial statement is one that refers to a group of companies, i.e. to a parent company and its subsidiaries. The main components of consolidated financial statements are: an income statement; a statement of recognized income and expense or a statement of changes in equity; a balance sheet; a cash flow statement; and pages and pages of detailed notes, including a list of accounting policies. A consolidated income statement shows the results of the operations of a group of companies over a period (usually one year). A consolidated balance sheet shows the financial position of a group of companies at a particular date. A consolidated cash flow statement shows the cash flows of a group for a period. The income statement and balance sheet (and sometimes other statements) of the parent company are also provided. A list of principal subsidiaries, their countries of incorporation and their role within the group and whether or not they are wholly owned is usually included in the notes.

The financial statements provide detailed data for the current year and the year preceding. Figures for other years can be accessed in previous reports but most listed companies summarize the most significant figures for, typically, the last five years.

The last item in many annual reports is a page of shareholder information. This usually comprises a list of important dates (e.g. the dates on which dividends are paid) and an analysis of who holds shares in the company.

In the next few sections of this chapter we explain, always in the context of company annual reports:

• the different kinds of companies and company groups
• why their activities as disclosed in their financial statements are of interest not just to shareholders but also to many others

- how companies are governed
- how companies report on operations and finance in narrative form
- how companies report on social responsibility
- how company legislation and other rules have been affected by the UK's membership of the European Union and by globalization.

COMPANIES AND COMPANY GROUPS

The chief characteristics of a limited liability company are: a corporate personality distinct from that of its owners or shareholders; the limiting of the liability of the shareholders to the amount invested (which is not the case for a sole trader or partnership without limited liability, where personal assets are available to pay business debts); and, in principle at least, a perpetual life – companies are born but they do not have to die of old age.

It was not until 1844 that incorporation became possible other than by the slow and difficult processes of a special Act of Parliament or a Royal Charter. It took another eleven years for registration to be linked with limited liability, by the Limited Liability Act 1855. The foundations of modern British company law (and also that of Australia, Canada, India, Ireland, Malaysia, New Zealand, Singapore, South Africa and many other Commonwealth or former Commonwealth countries) were laid in the Companies Act 1862. The law has been continually revised since. The most recent Companies Act is that of 2006, which is a result of a thorough review of the law by a committee appointed by the Department of Trade and Industry (DTI) and also owes much to the company law harmonization programme of the European Union. The longest Act of Parliament on the statute book, it has 1,300 sections and 16 schedules.

At 31 March 2006 there were about 2,130,200 companies registered in Great Britain, of which about 11,500 (0.5 per cent) were public companies and about 2,118,700 (99.5 per cent) were private companies. All must file certain documents periodically with the Registrar of Companies. In 2005–06 about 372,000 new companies were registered. A public company is one whose certificate of incorporation states that it is such, whose name ends with the words 'public limited company' or 'plc' (or, optionally, 'ccc' for companies registered in Wales) and which has a minimum allotted share capital of £50,000. Any company which is not a public company is a private company. A private company's name ends in 'Limited' or 'Ltd' (optionally 'cyf' for companies registered as Welsh companies). Private companies are not permitted to issue shares or debentures to the public. (Share capital and debentures are explained in Chapter 2.)

A public company does not have to make an issue of shares or debentures, it simply has the right to do so. Thus only about 2,650 UK public companies are listed (quoted) on the London Stock Exchange (LSE) and the division between private and public companies is not the same as that between listed companies and unlisted companies. It is a necessary but not a sufficient condition for listing that the company be a public company. Companies that are listed on a stock exchange are subject to the regulations of the Financial Services Authority (FSA), set up in 2000 to regulate the securities markets. A division of the FSA, the UK Listing Authority (UKLA), maintains the Official List of companies listed on the LSE and controls and monitors all listings. As will be seen in Chapter 4, neither the FSA nor the LSE plays a direct role in setting or monitoring financial reporting standards.

The Companies Act also classifies some private companies as small or medium-sized, using as criteria balance sheet total, turnover and the average number of employees. Small and medium-sized companies are exempted from filing certain data with the Registrar of Companies. As noted in Chapter 2, listed companies have the option to send summary financial statements to their shareholders. A summary financial statement is not necessarily a simplified statement or one that is easier to understand. This option has been taken up only by companies with a very large number of shareholders.

There is no limit to the number of shareholders that a company can have. Not all of them are individual persons. According to the share ownership surveys carried out by the Office for National Statistics, the percentage of persons investing in shares directly or indirectly through unit trusts fell from 26% in 1990, to 20% in 1998, to 15% by 2002. Continuing trends have been the growth of shareholdings by foreign investors (12% in 1990, 28% in 1998, 33% in 2004), and holdings by financial institutions such as pension funds and insurance companies (33% in 2004, down from a peak of 52% in 1991 as holdings by foreign investors have increased). Privatization, i.e. the selling-off of state-owned businesses such as public utilities, from the 1980s onwards increased in the short run the number of shares held by individuals, but many of them later sold out, and some companies have deliberately tried to reduce the number of their small shareholders. Nevertheless, companies formed by the privatization of former nationalized industries typically have the most shareholders. At 31 December 2005, for example, BG had 809,130 shareholders.

Privatization has opened companies up to foreign ownership and many public utilities are now owned by non-British companies. This is one of the reasons for the increasing foreign ownership of British companies. Many of the latter, of course, are themselves multinational companies that have invested heavily overseas. The UK is second only to the US in outward foreign direct investment, i.e. investment in a foreign enterprise with the intention of acquiring control or a significant influence. Some companies have more assets, sales and employees overseas than in the UK. BP and Vodafone are examples from contrasting industries.

Some companies voluntarily disclose shareholder statistics. These may sometimes be difficult to interpret because of shares held in the names of nominees rather than the beneficial holders. At 25 February 2006, Tesco had 293,251 shareholders. Only 6.4% were institutional shareholders but they held 92.48% of the shares; 18.45% of the shareholders were employees, holding 1.68% of the shares. Other individuals made up 75.15% of the number of shareholders and 5.84% of the shareholdings. The average individual shareholding was under 2,200 shares and the average institutional shareholding about 389,000 shares. Shareholdings of 3 per cent or over must be declared to a company by law. For example, Centrica's Directors' Report discloses that the Legal & General Group, Barclays and Petronas (a Malaysian company) each held just over 4 per cent of its shares at 31 December 2005.

The dominant form of business enterprise in the UK is not the individual undertaking but a group of undertakings (most but not necessarily all of which are companies) headed by a parent company. The parent controls subsidiaries. It may also significantly influence (but not control) other companies called associates. 'Associates' are distinguished from 'joint ventures', which are controlled jointly by two or more companies. It is possible for a subsidiary itself to have subsidiaries. These are the sub-subsidiaries of the first parent. In the illustration, A plc is the parent, B Ltd is its subsidiary and C Ltd is its sub-subsidiary. Note that although A plc controls C Ltd, its interest in its shares is only 48 per cent, that is, 80 per cent of 60 per cent. Some parent companies exist purely to hold shares in operating subsidiaries. Other parents are operating companies as well as holding shares in subsidiaries.

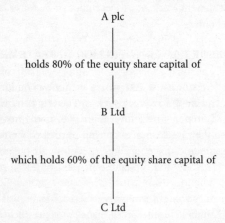

A plc

|

holds 80% of the equity share capital of

|

B Ltd

|

which holds 60% of the equity share capital of

|

C Ltd

The parent–subsidiary relationship is very common and practically all the company annual reports that the reader is likely to be interested in will be those of *groups* of companies. Just as there are small and medium-sized companies, there are also small and medium-sized groups. It is possible for subsidiaries to hold shares in each other, but the Companies Act makes it illegal, with minor exceptions, for a subsidiary to hold shares in its parent company.

The annual reports that we shall be concerned with, then, will be those of groups or sub-groups of companies. The parent company will usually be a plc. Other members of the group will be British public or private companies or companies incorporated overseas. All are likely to have share capital. It is worth noting in passing that not all companies do have share capital. This explains why auditors report to the 'members' of a company rather than to the 'shareholders'. Some companies are 'limited by guarantee', i.e. the members have undertaken to contribute a fixed amount to the assets of the company in the event of its being wound up. Network Rail is an example. A company limited by guarantee may be formed as or may become a community interest company ('CIC'). Some companies are even unlimited; since these have the privilege of not publishing their financial statements, they are not relevant to this book. There are also limited liability partnerships (LLPs). These are popular with professional firms, including the large auditing firms. Unlike ordinary partnerships, all the partners in LLPs have limited liability and their financial statements have to be published and audited.

USERS OF COMPANY FINANCIAL STATEMENTS

The annual reports of listed companies are formally addressed only to shareholders, and many lay great stress on 'creating shareholder value'. Nevertheless, the reports are also of interest to many non-shareholders and in practice they are treated as general purpose documents available to whoever wants to use them. These users include potential investors, employees, loan creditors, financial analysts, business contacts (customers and suppliers), government agencies and the public. Many users are also likely to be at the same time 'stakeholders' in the company. Stakeholders can be classified into primary stakeholders (the shareholders), who have an ownership interest in the company; secondary stakeholders (e.g. loan creditors, employees, business contacts and tax collectors) with a financial but not an ownership interest; and tertiary stakeholders, who have no direct financial interest, but are affected, or believe themselves to be affected, by the way in which the company's resources are managed (e.g. persons affected by pollution caused or allegedly caused by the company's activities). Some companies prepare special reports for some of these stakeholders, some of which may be distributed with the annual report. These include reports for employees (who may of course also be shareholders), which may present information in a simpler and more graphic form, or emphasize valued added (see Chapters 2 and 6) rather than profit. Many other users and stakeholders could also benefit from simplified statements and different ways of presenting information.

CORPORATE GOVERNANCE

Listed companies are owned by shareholders, but most shareholders take no part in the formulation of company strategy or the day-to-day operations of the company. These are delegated to a board of directors, members of which whilst typically holding only a very small percentage of the shares effectively control the company. Boards are given considerable freedom in the way companies are run and, except in times of crisis, are subject to very little interference from the shareholders. This separation of ownership from control gives rise to what is known as an 'agency problem'. The directors are the 'agents' of the shareholders who are their 'principals', but it is very difficult for the latter to hold the former to account.

These problems of accountability are well recognized and have been addressed in a number of reports in the UK, out of which has been developed what is known as the Combined Code on Corporate Governance, which is the responsibility of the Financial Reporting Council (FRC) (see Chapter 4). The most recent edition of the Code was issued in 2006. The Code is voluntary but is backed up by the rules of the UK Listing Authority. It operates on a 'comply or explain' basis, i.e. listed companies which do not comply with one or more of its provisions must explain in their annual report why they are not doing so. The Code requires, *inter alia*, disclosures relating to directors' remuneration (see below), audit committees and internal controls (see Chapter 3), and a statement that the company is a going concern.

Annual reports therefore include a section on Corporate Governance which sets out the roles and responsibilities of the chairman, the chief executive (sometimes known as the managing director), the executive directors and the non-executive directors. The full board, comprising both the executives and the non-executives, is usually responsible for such matters as the formulation of corporate strategy, approval of acquisitions of other companies and of major capital expenditure, and treasury policy. The executive directors are responsible for implementation and the control of day-to-day operations. Non-executives are typically of two kinds: those with long experience and knowledge of the group in question, and those from outside the group whose function is to bring a wider perspective and/or specialized knowledge and contacts not available from within the group.

Directors' remuneration is determined by a remuneration committee, which usually comprises the chairman and the non-executive directors. Detailed disclosure is required by company legislation and the report of the committee usually covers several pages. Directors of listed companies are typically not only well paid, but paid in an astonishing number of different ways. Remuneration covers not just salaries but also fees, bonuses, expenses, allowances chargeable to UK income tax, the estimated money value of benefits in kind, pensions and retirement benefits, share options, and compensation for loss of office. The complexity of the forms of remuneration reflects attempts to reward directors for performance and to minimize taxation. Disclosure is also required of directors' service contracts, shareholdings in the company, and of loans and other transactions involving directors. How to account for share options has been highly controversial and is discussed in Chapter 2.

NARRATIVE REPORTING: THE BUSINESS REVIEW

The Companies Act 2006 requires for the first time that companies publish a 'business review'. This is an example of narrative reporting, the presentation of financial and other information as a continuous narrative rather than as a series of financial statements. The Companies Act requirement has been anticipated by companies and the accountancy profession by the publication of an operating and financial review and (by some companies) a corporate social responsibility review.

The operating and financial review (OFR) provides in a mixture of words and figures an explanation of and an analysis by the directors of a company's performance and financial position. Unlike the financial statements, which it both complements and supplements, it is intended to have a forward-looking orientation. The contents have not been regulated in detail, but the Accounting Standards Board (see Chapter 4) has issued a non-mandatory guidance statement. Typical contents of the OFR are a statement on strategy, a discussion of current and future events, and operating and financial data. For example, BPI in its 2005 OFR confirms its intention to remain 'a focused polythene film and bag business'; explains the impact of, and its reaction to, increases in the price of raw materials and environmental legislation; discusses performance both by product and by geographical area; summarizes key financial figures for the year; outlines the group's treasury policy; explains the impact of the first-time application of IFRS; and confirms that the group is a going concern. In its 2006 report, Tesco includes a section of key performance indicators derived from the 'balanced scorecard' approach that they use internally and from measures of return on shareholder investment. A balanced scorecard is a reporting technique which gives an equal emphasis to financial and non-financial measures of performance. Tesco also spells out in detail, both in the OFR and in the report on corporate governance, the risks and uncertainties of doing business and the management policies for dealing with them.

Not all the costs and benefits arising from the operations of a company appear in its own accounting records. Those that do not are 'social' costs and benefits arising from what are known as 'externalities'. An obvious example of a social cost is the emission of greenhouse gases by a company factory. There is no general legal obligation for companies to publish in their annual reports the social costs and benefits arising from their operations or the costs to themselves of socially responsible actions. Although there is no consensus as to what these actions comprise, they probably include at least the following: control of pollution; energy conservation; health and safety measures; product safety; community involvement; employment of disabled persons; and donations to charities. The last two are required to be disclosed in the Directors' Report.

Companies have reported on social responsibility in their annual reports in different ways. Some (e.g. Johnson Matthey in 2006) do so as part of the OFR; some (e.g. BPI, 2005) devote a separate section of the annual report to it; others (e.g. Scottish and Southern Energy, 2005) refer readers to a separate publication which is summarized in the annual report. The contents of a corporate social responsibility (CSR) report have not been regulated, but the following topics are typical: health and safety; energy; the environment; relevant legislation; employment policies; education; charitable support. CSR reports are a mixture of 'hard' (quantitative) and 'soft' (qualitative) information. Reporting on the environment is colloquially known as 'green' reporting.

Many companies circulate a simplified version of the annual report to their employees. This may include a value added statement, which is essentially a reworking of the income statement from a stakeholder point of view. There is more explanation and discussion of value added statements in Chapter 6. Employee reports should be distinguished from employment reports, which are reports about employees as distinct from reports to employees.

THE EUROPEAN UNION AND GLOBALIZATION

Two of the most important political and economic developments relevant to companies in the last few decades have been the formation and gradual enlargement of the European Union (EU) and the globalization of trade and finance. Both have strongly influenced financial reporting in the UK. At the same time, UK accountants have been active both in Europe and internationally. Many amendments to British company law from the 1980s onwards were the result of implementing the company law 'directives' of the EU. Directives form part of UK law only when they have been incorporated into domestic legislation. The most important directives from the point of view of financial reporting were the fourth (on the financial statements of individual companies), the seventh (on the financial statements of groups) and the eighth (on auditors). It was the fourth directive that introduced into UK legislation standardized formats for financial statements (see Chapter 4) and the three-tier classification into large, medium-sized and small companies already referred to. Globalization has to some extent meant Americanization, and American financial reporting rules and practices have become increasingly well known and increasingly influential in the UK. This influence has been tempered by the growth of international standards.

In the same year (1973) that the UK joined the EU, the world's leading accountancy bodies set up the International Accounting Standards Committee (IASC), now replaced by the International Accounting Standards Board (IASB). The IASC issued international accounting standards (now included in international financial reporting standards or IFRS), whose content was mainly influenced by accounting standards in the US and the UK. There was at first some tension between continental European and international rules, but the growing need of large continental European companies to raise money on international capital markets eventually led to a recommendation by the European Commission that the consolidated financial statements of listed companies, but not necessarily any other statements, should be required to follow IFRS. This was achieved by an EU regulation of 2002 that came into force in 2005. There is further discussion of this in Chapter 4.

INTERIM REPORTS AND PRELIMINARY ANNOUNCEMENTS

The annual report is not the only source of information about a listed company's financial statements. For stock markets hungry for new information, twelve months is far too long to wait. Two other important sources are interim reports and preliminary announcements. The UK Listing Authority requires listed companies to issue interim reports on a half-yearly basis. Some UK companies, especially those which also have a listing in the US, issue quarterly reports. Interim reports are not audited but may be subject to an independent review (falling short of a full audit) by the company's auditors. The main content of interim reports is condensed versions of the financial statements and the notes thereto. Many companies also provide reports from the chairman and/or the chief executive and an operating and financial review.

A preliminary announcement is the announcement by a company of its annual results before the full annual report is made available. Preliminary announcements are regulated by the Listing Authority. They are not audited but are 'agreed' with the auditors before publication. The content is similar to that of the interim report.

The Financial Statements

> The statements was interesting but tough.
> Mark Twain, *The Adventures of Huckleberry Finn*, Chapter 17

TYPES OF FINANCIAL STATEMENTS

Many types of financial statements can be drawn up and not all of them are published in annual reports. This chapter looks more closely at those that are, with the emphasis on consolidated financial statements and the notes related thereto. Companies usually place the consolidated income statements first but for purposes of exposition it is easier to begin with the consolidated balance sheet. The statements are therefore discussed in the following order:

- consolidated balance sheet
- consolidated income statement
- consolidated statement of recognized income and expense / consolidated statement of changes in equity
- consolidated cash flow statement.

In principle, all numbers in the financial statements are intended to be relevant to the price of a company's shares. Research has shown, however, that some of the numbers have more value relevance, as it is termed, than others.

CONSOLIDATED BALANCE SHEET: ASSETS, LIABILITIES AND SHAREHOLDERS' EQUITY

The consolidated balance sheet is a statement of the financial position of a group of companies as if it were one company. For this reason it is sometimes referred to as the group balance sheet.

International financial reporting standards (IFRS) do not mandate a particular form of presentation but do require the disclosure of certain items on the face of the balance sheet or in the notes. As a result of the EU's fourth directive on company financial statements, UK GAAP (generally accepted accounting practice) is more prescriptive, and *parent company* balance sheets are more standardized in form, if, as is permitted, they follow UK GAAP (see Chapter 4). Some UK listed companies draw up their consolidated balance sheets in accordance with IFRS but their parent company balance sheets in accordance with UK GAAP. All company balance sheets, however, whether parent or consolidated, are built up from three main categories: assets, liabilities and shareholders' equity (sometimes called shareholders' funds). Assets are defined by IFRS and UK GAAP as resources controlled by an enterprise as a result of past events and from which future economic benefits are expected to flow to the enterprise. In most cases, but not all, control derives from legal ownership. Liabilities are defined by IFRS and UK GAAP as the present obligations of an enterprise arising from past events, the settlement of which is expected to result in an outflow from the enterprise of resources embodying economic benefits. The relationship between the assets, liabilities and shareholders' equity can be looked at either from the point of view of the shareholders (a 'proprietary' approach) or from the point of view of the company as a whole (an 'entity' approach). Two forms of a fundamental balance sheet identity can thus be derived:

Proprietary: assets − liabilities = shareholders' equity

Entity: assets = shareholders' equity + liabilities

Very broadly, all that is being said is that, firstly, what a company has *less* what a company owes is equal to the value of the shareholders' equity invested in it, and that, secondly, what a company has is financed partly by the owners (the shareholders) and partly by outsiders (the liabilities).

Either way a balance sheet must, by definition, balance. The useful accounting technique known as double entry ('debits' and 'credits') is based on these same identities (see Appendix A).

As we shall see in the next few sections, these categories can each be subdivided. In particular, a distinction is drawn between current and non-current items. Shareholders' equity can be subdivided into share capital and reserves; assets into non-current assets and current assets; and liabilities into current liabilities and non-current liabilities.

Many British companies adopt a proprietary approach, with some rearrangement of the subdivisions to emphasize the current/non-current distinction:

> Non-current assets + (current assets − current liabilities) − non-current liabilities = shareholders' equity

For example, BPI's 2005 consolidated balance sheet can be summarized as below:

	£m
Non-current assets	93.5
Current assets	119.4
Current liabilities	75.5
Net current assets	43.9
Total assets less current liabilities	137.4
Non-current liabilities	100.2
Net assets	37.2
Parent shareholders' equity	37.0
Minority interests	0.2
Total equity	37.2

Broadly, the total equity is represented by the sum of the total assets net of the current liabilities less the non-current liabilities. Total equity is divided into parent shareholders' equity and minority interests, the latter representing that part of the subsidiaries' assets and liabilities that are owned by outside shareholders.

CURRENT ASSETS, CURRENT LIABILITIES AND WORKING CAPITAL

Current assets are essentially those assets expected to be realized, sold or consumed within one year or within a company's normal operating cycle. They consist mainly of cash, financial assets, trade and other receivables (also known as debtors), and inventories (also known as stocks). Cash and cash equivalents include money on deposit with a maturity of three months or less. UK-based multinationals hold cash in several currencies, not just sterling. The composition and classification of financial assets are explained below (pp. 23–5). Receivables are shown net of an allowance for debts that are irrecoverable, i.e. net of doubtful as well as bad debts. Inventories in the case of a manufacturing company comprise raw materials, work in progress (i.e. partly completed manufactured goods) and finished goods. They are stated at the lower of cost and net realizable value (i.e. expected selling price net of selling expenses). 'Cost' is not unambiguous. Inventories in the UK are usually valued on a 'first in first out' (FIFO) basis. An alternative assumption, 'last in last out' (LILO), is popular in the US for tax reasons, but is not allowed in the UK. The cost of finished goods and work in progress is the sum of direct materials, direct labour and those production overheads that have been incurred in bringing the inventories to their present location and condition. It does not include administrative and distribution overheads.

Current liabilities are essentially those that will have to be settled within one year or within the company's normal operating cycle. They include bank overdrafts, other loans and borrowings due and payable within one year of the date of the balance sheet, trade and other payables (usually by far the largest item and also referred to as trade and other creditors), and current tax liabilities. They do not include a final dividend recommended by the directors to be paid to the shareholders, since this will not become a liability of the company until it is formally approved by the shareholders at the annual general meeting. Deducting current liabilities from current assets gives net current assets, also referred to as net working capital or (more usually) just working capital. The relationship between current assets and current liabilities is very important and is discussed in Chapter 7 on liquidity.

NON-CURRENT ASSETS

Non-current assets (also known as fixed assets) comprise all assets that are not current assets. They include those held for use on a continuing basis for the purpose of the company's activities, such as factories and the head office building. Inventories, for example, are not regarded as non-current assets since they are acquired either for immediate resale (e.g. this book as sold by a bookshop) or as raw materials for use in manufacturing operations, or are the finished or partly finished ('work in progress') results of such operations. It is the nature of the business not of the asset that determines whether assets are non-current or not. Delivery vans, for example, are the non-current assets of publishers but the current assets of companies who manufacture or retail them.

The 2005 consolidated balance sheet of Scottish and Southern Energy (SSE) lists the following non-current assets:

	£m
Property, plant and equipment	4,646.6
Intangible assets	
Goodwill	293.4
Other intangible assets	297.2
Investments in associates and jointly controlled entities	703.1
Other investments	3.3
Retirement benefit assets	90.2
Deferred tax assets	86.0
Derivative financial assets	24.8
	6,144.6

PROPERTY, PLANT AND EQUIPMENT

The largest non-current asset of a manufacturing company, and the easiest to understand, is usually property, plant and equipment (PPE, also known as tangible fixed assets). Property, plant and equipment may be defined as tangible assets held by an enterprise for use in the production or supply of goods or services, for rental to others, or for administrative purposes, and which are expected to be used during more than one accounting period. Most companies state this asset at cost, less accumulated depreciation and accumulated impairment losses (see below). 'Cost' in this context usually means the historical cost of acquisition or manufacture (if the asset was made by the company for its own use). Historical cost has been favoured by accountants because it is thought to be easily verifiable by an independent third party such as an auditor and hence reliable. It can, however, get seriously out of line with current values in times of inflation. Land and buildings are sometimes revalued, but not other items of property, plant and equipment. With two exceptions, property, plant and equipment must be depreciated, whether it is carried at cost or a valuation. The exceptions are freehold land and investment property. Investment property comprises land and buildings held for capital appreciation or to earn rentals. Such property is shown as a separate item from PPE. It can be carried in the balance sheet at either cost or at fair value. If fair value is chosen (as is common in the UK) the property is not depreciated but the changes in fair value each year must be recognized in the income statement.

Companies analyse the composition of property, plant and equipment in the notes. That of Centrica is quite complicated: land and buildings; plant, equipment and vehicles and office equipment; power generation; and (by far the largest item) storage, exploration and production. BPI's split is much simpler: land and buildings; and plant and equipment.

DEPRECIATION, AMORTIZATION AND IMPAIRMENT

In an accounting context, depreciation means the systematic allocation of the cost or revalued amount (net of residual value at the end of its life) of a tangible non-current asset over its estimated useful life. As noted above, freehold land is not depreciated, being deemed to have an infinite life and not to be used up in operations. BPI, Centrica and SSE, like many other companies, use the straight line method of depreciation. Under this method the cost less residual value is divided by the number of years of its estimated useful life. If for example a machine costs £1,200 and is expected to have a residual value of £130 at the end of an estimated useful life of ten years, the annual depreciation will be £1,070/10 = £107.

The charging of depreciation simultaneously reduces the recorded amount of the non-current asset and reduces the operating profit. The amounts for non-current assets in the consolidated balance sheet are net of all accumulated depreciation and impairment losses, not only of the current year but of all previous years since the purchase of the assets concerned.

Depreciation is neither a cash inflow nor a cash outflow. The cash outflow takes place when the property, plant and equipment is purchased. It would be double counting to regard each year's depreciation as a further cash outflow. Charging depreciation does, however, reduce reported profits and may thus limit what is regarded as an acceptable cash outflow of dividends. For monetary assets and intangible assets the term 'amortization' is normally used instead of depreciation.

Impairment is different from depreciation and amortization. It is not a systematic allocation but a recognition of decrease in the recoverable amount of an asset, either by sale or in use. Calculating impairment is a less mechanical procedure than calculating depreciation. The recoverable amount is the higher of net realizable value and value in use. The latter is usually higher, because otherwise the asset would have been sold. It is estimated by discounting the future cash flows expected from the asset. Discounting reduces the amount of each cash flow by the use of a rate of interest. The calculation of value in use can be difficult and there are obvious problems of reliability. However, the resulting figures can be highly relevant, especially for intangible assets, as the next section demonstrates.

GOODWILL AND OTHER INTANGIBLE ASSETS

Intangible assets are non-monetary assets without physical substance. Some intangibles – for example, brands, patents, trade marks, copyrights, software – can be separately identified and may be extremely valuable. In an information-based economy increasingly based on trading services rather than physical products, the relative importance of intangibles has grown in recent years. The intangible assets of Cadbury Schweppes, for instance, accounted for nearly three-quarters of its non-current assets in its 2005 balance sheet, and those of Unilever comprised nearly two-thirds.

Goodwill is the term used for intangible assets that cannot be separately identified. A company is not just a collection of tangible assets. It is, or should be, a going concern whose total value, by reason of its proven ability to earn profits, is greater than the sum of its parts. It is the difference between that total value and the sum of the parts (including identifiable intangibles) which constitutes goodwill. Unfortunately, goodwill is difficult to value reliably except at the date of purchase. Goodwill internally generated by a company is not recognized as an asset. The goodwill that is recognized is that which arises on the acquisition of a subsidiary whose assets are included in the consolidated balance sheet. It represents the excess of the cost of shares in the subsidiary companies over the fair value of their net tangible and identifiable intangible assets at the date of acquisition. That is, the parent company was willing to pay more to purchase the company than the sum of its tangible and identifiable intangible assets. The accounting treatment of goodwill has been controversial and has changed several times in recent decades. Under IFRS, goodwill is not subject to amortization but must be tested for impairment of its value at least annually and its value written down accordingly if necessary. Its value must not be written up. Impairment tests are not easy to make and can be unreliable. However, they may be highly relevant and significant in size: Vodafone recognized a goodwill impairment loss of £23,515 million in its 2005 financial statements, related mainly to its takeover in 2000 of the German company Mannesmann.

All identifiable intangibles are tested for impairment losses annually, and whenever there is an indication of possible impairment. Those with finite lives (e.g. copyrights) are amortized over their estimated economic lives; those with indefinite lives (e.g. most brands) are not amortized. Some intangibles are difficult to identify. For example, the cost of researching a new product is not treated as an asset; the cost of developing the product, however, is treated as an asset if it meets certain criteria. The costs of research and development must be disclosed whether or not they are capitalized. Academic studies suggest that the amount of R & D is a highly value relevant figure.

INVESTMENTS IN ASSOCIATES AND
JOINT VENTURES

Associates are companies or other enterprises in which a group has an equity interest that gives it the ability to exercise significant influence. Significant influence is a power to participate in financial and operating decisions which falls short of control or joint control. It is presumed to exist (although the presumption can be rebutted) where the investor company holds 20 per cent or more of the voting power of the investee. In the consolidated balance sheet associates are valued at cost plus a proportionate share of the associate's reserves and retained earnings since the date of acquisition, less any impairment in the value of the investments. This accounting treatment, which differs from that used for subsidiaries, is known as the equity method. It is also referred to as one-line consolidation. In the *parent* company balance sheet, shares in both subsidiaries and associates are valued at cost less any impairment losses. The shares of subsidiaries are, however, eliminated from the *consolidated* balance sheet and replaced by their underlying assets and liabilities.

A joint venture is a contractual arrangement, requiring unanimous decisions, whereby two or more parties undertake an economic activity that is subject to joint control. There are three forms of joint ventures: jointly controlled operations; jointly controlled assets; and jointly controlled entities. Jointly controlled entities may be incorporated or unincorporated. They are usually accounted for by the equity method in the UK but may also be accounted for by proportional consolidation.

FINANCIAL ASSETS

Financial assets comprise principally cash, accounts receivable and investments in, and loans to, other companies. They are classified into four categories: held for trading, held to maturity, loans and receivables, and available for sale. Financial assets held for trading include not only investments acquired for sale in the near term but also, as explained below, derivatives. Financial assets held to maturity are those investments, other than derivatives, that a company intends and is able to hold on to. Loans and receivables are non-derivative financial assets with fixed or determinable payments that are not quoted on an active market. Financial assets available for sale are investments designated by the directors as such and not falling into the other three categories. Which category a financial asset falls into determines the way in which it is valued in the balance sheet and the extent to which fluctuations in its value affect reported income. Financial assets held to maturity and loans and receivables are stated in the balance sheet at amortized cost. The amortization is based on the effective rate of interest at the date of acquisition. Unlike property, plant and equipment, the amortized cost of a financial asset can increase, as well as decrease, over time as the asset approaches maturity. Both financial assets held for trading and financial assets available for sale are stated at fair value in the balance sheet, but there are significant differences in their accounting treatment. Financial assets held for trading are current assets and are 'marked to market', i.e. changes in fair values are passed through the income statement and affect reported profit. Financial assets available for sale are non-current assets whose changes in fair value are instead passed through the statement of recognized gains and losses (or the statement of changes in equity) and do not affect reported profit. It is a weakness of these complicated rules that the categorization of a financial asset depends in part on directors' intentions, giving them an opportunity to avoid volatility in reported income and in balance sheet values. This is of most importance to those companies, such as financial institutions, whose assets are mainly financial.

For some companies, such as Centrica, the most important financial assets are derivatives. Derivatives are financial assets or liabilities that derive their value from an underlying item such as a share price or an interest rate. They include financial options and forward exchange contracts. For example, a company may buy an option that entitles it to purchase shares in another company at a fixed price at any time within a specified period. Whether or not it will exercise the option will depend upon the market price of the share during that period. The rules relating to the accounting treatment of derivatives of this kind are extremely complex, but in general derivatives are recorded at fair value, with changes in fair value taken to the income statement.

There are many risks pertaining to financial instruments. For example, foreign currency exchange rates, interest rates and market prices are all subject to fluctuation; parties to financial instruments may be unable to meet their obligations; expected cash flows may not happen. Companies are required to explain in their annual reports the extent to which they are exposed to risks of this kind. These risks also explain why companies purchase hedging instruments. A hedging instrument is an asset or a liability, changes in the fair value of which or in the cash flows generated by it are expected to offset changes in the fair value or cash flows of the hedged item. For example, a UK company which has to pay an invoice in US dollars in three months time may, in order to protect itself against fluctuations in the sterling/dollar exchange rate, hedge by buying dollars at today's forward exchange rate for delivery in three months time. If the dollar then falls against sterling, the fair value of the hedging instrument will fall and the company will record a loss on an instrument which it purchased to protect itself against a loss. For this reason special rules apply to hedging instruments. Under what is known as hedge accounting the loss can, subject to certain conditions, be passed not through the income statement but through the statement of recognized income and expense (SORIE) or the statement of changes in equity.

NON-CURRENT FINANCIAL LIABILITIES

Non-current financial liabilities comprise principally borrowings and provisions.

The most straightforward item amongst the non-current liabilities is loans and other borrowings. They represent the extent to which the group, not wishing to obtain further long-term funds from its shareholders, has borrowed from outsiders. Companies distinguish between those loans and borrowings falling due within one year, which they include under current liabilities (£6.8 million for BPI at 31 December 2005), and loans and borrowings falling due after more than one year (£41.2 million for BPI). The latter are sometimes further classified into, e.g. between one year and two years, between two and five years, and five years or more.

Banks are an obvious source of outside finance, but bank loans and overdrafts are not the only forms of borrowing. A 'debenture' is a document providing evidence of a long-term borrowing or loan. Debentures are usually but not necessarily secured on the assets of the company, in which case they may be known as mortgage debentures. If a company fails in its obligation to pay interest or repay the loan, the secured property of the company can be sold in order to provide the necessary funds. The term 'unsecured debenture' is unusual, unsecured loan usually being preferred. The term 'debenture stock' is used when a company, instead of issuing individual debentures, creates one loan fund to be divided among a class of lenders, each of whom will receive a debenture stock certificate. Companies may, and often do, make more than one issue of debentures, the terms of issue, and, in particular, the rate of interest varying according to the financial circumstances of the time. Such issues may be made at par (i.e. at face value), at a discount (less than face value) or at a premium (more than face value). Issue at a discount increases the effective interest rate payable; issue at a premium (which is rare) decreases it. Issues are often made at a discount in order to keep the interest rate on the par value (known as the coupon rate) a reasonably round figure, while allowing the effective rate to be adjusted more finely.

Debentures and loans may be secured by a fixed charge on a particular asset or by a floating charge on all the assets or particular classes of asset. A floating charge, unlike a fixed charge, allows a company to dispose of the assets charged in the usual course of business without obtaining special permission from the lender. Inventory is a particularly suitable asset to be charged in this manner. If assets are, or may be, used as security for more than one loan, it is necessary to state the order of priority of the lenders (for example debenture stock may be stated to be secured by a *first* floating charge).

Some debentures are irredeemable – that is, they will never have to be repaid (unless the company is wound up) – but most are redeemable. It is common not only to specify the latest date, but also to give the company the power to redeem earlier if it so wishes. This is especially useful if debentures are issued in times of high interest rates and there is an expectation of lower rates later.

In principle there is a clear distinction between borrowings and shareholders' equity. In practice, especially in recent years, the distinction has become blurred by the issue of compound financial instruments: securities with the characteristics of both debt and equity. These are required to be split into their component parts. There has also been an increase in 'off balance sheet finance': attempts to borrow in such a way that the debt does not appear as a balance sheet item. For example, if an asset is leased instead of bought it will appear in the balance sheet if it is a 'finance lease', but not if it is an 'operating lease'. Both leasing and off balance sheet financing in general are discussed further in Chapter 8.

How much to borrow and in what form to do so are vital matters for any company. These problems are also investigated in Chapter 8.

PROVISIONS

Provisions are liabilities that are uncertain in timing or amount. To be recognized in a balance sheet a provision must involve a probable outflow of resources whose amount can be reliably measured. This definition excludes both contingent liabilities (see the next section) and deferred taxation (discussed in Chapter 3). The most important provisions are those for pensions and other employee benefits, and those for restructuring.

Most listed companies operate pension plans or schemes for their employees. Some (although more in the US than in the UK) may commit themselves to paying their employees' medical bills after retirement. From the company's point of view, pensions and other employee benefits are equivalent to a salary with a postponed payment date. They are liabilities but ones for which the company can only estimate the date and the amount of payment. There are two main types of company pension plan in the UK: the defined contribution plan and the defined benefit plan. Under the former, the company pays specified amounts of money into the plan, which is run by a pension trust independent of the company. The company has no further obligation. Under a defined benefit plan, the obligation of the employer is not fixed, the amount of pensions potentially payable typically depending on the employees' final salaries and on how long they live after retirement. To meet the pensions, a company may build up an investment fund outside the company.

Companies estimate their pension obligation at balance sheet date. Since the obligation refers to amounts payable over many years in the future, it is discounted to its present value by the use of a discount rate based on current market interest rates. The difference between the pension obligation at the beginning of the year and at the end of a year is made up of two main items: the net annual cost of servicing and financing the pensions; and actuarial gains and losses. The former is charged as an expense in the income statement. Actuarial gains and losses are difficult to estimate, and may be large and volatile; companies have therefore been reluctant to charge them against current income. They have the option to pass them through the statement of recognized income and expense (or statement of changes in equity) so that they do not affect the profit for the year.

When a company acquires another company it may propose to incur considerable costs in reorganizing and restructuring it. The acquiror may therefore set up a 'provision for restructuring'. This results not in a charge in the income statement but in an increase in the figure for goodwill on consolidation. In order to prevent over-enthusiastic provisioning the creation of restructuring provisions is constrained by complicated rules.

It is important to note that the creation of provisions does not automatically involve the setting aside of money or investments (perhaps in a 'sinking fund') to meet such costs when they fall due.

CONTINGENT LIABILITIES AND CONTINGENT ASSETS

Contingent liabilities are of two types. The first is possible obligations that arise from past events and whose existence will be confirmed only by the occurrence or non-occurrence of one or more uncertain events that are not wholly within the control of the company. Strictly, this type of contingent liability is not a liability at all since it is a possible obligation not a present obligation. Common examples are the guarantee by the parent company of bank overdrafts of subsidiaries and recourse by a bank in relation to discounted bills of exchange. A more interesting example is that in BPI's 2005 annual report, relating to penalties that might be imposed for an alleged infringement of European competition law.

The second type of contingent liability is a present obligation that arises from past events where it is not probable that an outflow of resources will be required, or where the amount of the obligation cannot be measured with sufficient reliability. Although there is a present obligation, it is not a provision because it fails to meet one or more of the recognition criteria. Both types of contingent liability are disclosed in the notes, not in the financial statements themselves.

A contingent asset is a possible asset that arises from past events and whose existence will be confirmed only by the occurrence or non-occurrence of one or more uncertain future events not wholly within the control of the company. Contingent assets are disclosed in the notes where an inflow of benefits in the future is probable. An example is the possible receipt of damages of uncertain amount as a result of a court case already decided in favour of the company.

SHAREHOLDERS' EQUITY AND MINORITY INTERESTS

The equity section of a consolidated balance sheet is subdivided into share capital, reserves and minority interests. The first two constitute the parent company shareholders' equity; the last the equity in the group that relates to shareholders other than those of the parent company.

Shareholders differ from debenture and other loan holders in three main ways: they are members (owners) of the company, not lenders; they receive dividends (a share of the profits), not interest; and except in special circumstances, the cost of their shares will not be repaid (redeemed) to them by their company. Both the redemption of shares and the buying by a company of its own shares in the market are, however, allowable subject to certain restrictions. For example, BPI purchased 200,000 of its own shares in 2004 and in previous years redeemed and cancelled its preference shares (as indicated by the existence of a capital redemption reserve, see below).

There are two main types of shares: ordinary and preference. The difference between an ordinary shareholder and a preference shareholder is considerable. The latter is usually only entitled to a dividend at a fixed rate (8 per cent in the case of BP's cumulative first preference shares, for example) but has priority of repayment in the event of the company being wound up. This is not always so, however, and the exact rights must always be ascertained. Preference shares may be cumulative (as for those of BP) or non-cumulative. If a company misses a dividend on cumulative shares, it must carry it forward to a later year, and disclose any arrears of dividends in the notes. Non-cumulative preference dividends do not have to be carried forward. Some so-called preference shares, especially if they are redeemable, may be in reality not equity but either wholly debt or a compound of equity and liability. If the latter is the case, they must be split accordingly in the balance sheet.

The size of the dividends paid to ordinary shareholders varies according to the profits made by the company. During 2005, the directors of BPI declared an interim ordinary dividend of 7p per share and proposed a final dividend of 15p per share. The total ordinary dividend was thus 22p. The par or face value of the shares is 25p and the dividend could be described as a dividend of 88 per cent on the par value. More important to the investor is the relationship between the dividend and the current *market* price of the share. This is known as the dividend yield and is discussed in Chapter 8 in the context of earnings yields and price–earnings ratios. For the moment it should be noted that every share must have a par value (i.e. no-par-value shares are illegal) but that this is not necessarily the same as the issue price of the shares or their current market price. Once a share has been issued, its market price fluctuates from day to day in accordance with supply and demand. If the shares can be bought and sold on a stock exchange, the current market price can easily be found in the financial pages of a daily newspaper or on the internet. The most complete newspaper list is given in the *Financial Times*. The information given in that newspaper's daily share information service is further discussed in Chapter 8.

A company does not have to request full payment on its shares immediately. As at 31 December 2005 BPI had issued 25,894,393 ordinary shares (par value £6.5 million). All these shares are described as being allotted, called up and fully paid, i.e. the company does not have the right to call up any further amounts on them from the shareholders. Shares can be partly paid. For example, a 25p share could be payable 5p on application for the shares, a further 5p on allotment, when the directors decide to whom the shares are to be issued ('allotted'), and the remaining 15p in calls. Thus, in summary, one can distinguish issued, allotted, called up and paid up share capital. Most companies do not make substantial share issues on a regular basis, but the issued share capital of many listed companies may increase annually, by relatively small amounts, through issues to employee share schemes and dividend reinvestment schemes.

Employees, and directors in particular, may be paid in part by the giving to them of shares or options to buy shares. Share-based payments constitute both an expense and equity. BPI explains its accounting policy as follows:

The fair value of share options granted is calculated at grant date and the resulting cost is charged to the income statement over the vesting period of the options with a corresponding increase in equity. The value of the charge is adjusted to reflect expected and actual levels of options vesting.

Fair value in this context normally means the market price of the shares, but in some cases it may need to be estimated. By 'vesting period' is meant the period over which the employee performs the services which entitle him or her to exercise the option.

The other element of equity is 'reserves'. In its 2005 annual report, BPI lists share premium account, other reserves (capital redemption reserve, capital reserve, hedging reserve, foreign currency translation reserve) and retained earnings. A share premium arises when, as is common, shares are issued at more than their par value. Although a share premium cannot be distributed as a dividend it can be used to make a bonus or capitalization issue (see Chapter 8). A capital redemption reserve is created when shares are redeemed otherwise than out of a new issue of shares. A sum equal to the par value of the shares redeemed is transferred from retained earnings. A capital reserve may need to be created in a number of circumstances. BPI's arose on the acquisition of a subsidiary. A hedging reserve comprises changes in the fair value of hedging instruments related to forecast hedging transactions that have not yet occurred. The foreign exchange translation reserve comprises all foreign exchange translation differences arising from the translation of financial statements within the group not kept in sterling, and also from the translation of liabilities that hedge the company's net investment in foreign operations. Accounting for foreign exchange is discussed later in this chapter. A further type of reserve is an asset revaluation reserve. This offsets the increase in the recorded amount of an asset resulting from a revaluation.

Retained earnings in the consolidated balance sheet comprise those profits after tax which have not yet been paid out in dividends by the member companies in the group. The dividends distributed to the shareholders of BPI are paid by the parent company, not by the group (which is not a legal entity). The balance of retained earnings in a parent company balance sheet may be quite different from that in the consolidated balance sheet.

Reserves have many different origins, but none of them tells us anything about a company's resources of cash. To say that a company has large reserves is not the same thing as saying that the company has lots of cash. Reserves are part of equity. The accounting or balance sheet identity (p. 16) tells us that if a company has reserves it must have net assets of equal amount, but these assets may be of any kind (e.g. property, plant and equipment; inventories). It is perfectly possible (and often sensible) for a company to have both large reserves and a large bank overdraft.

Minority interest is the name given to that part of the equity which is not held by the shareholders of the parent company. It arises because some subsidiaries, although controlled by the parent company, are not fully owned. BPI, for example, owns only 75 per cent of its Hong Kong subsidiary. The minority interest in BPI's consolidated balance sheet comprises 25 per cent of the shareholders' equity of that subsidiary.

EVENTS AFTER THE BALANCE SHEET DATE

Important events may sometimes take place between the date of the balance sheet (e.g. 31 December 2006) and the date on which it is approved for publication by the board of directors (e.g. 9 March 2007). An event which does not provide additional evidence of conditions existing at the balance sheet date (e.g. the acquisition of a new subsidiary in February 2007) is known as a 'non-adjusting event'. A example of an 'adjusting event', one which would require the financial statements to be altered if the amount was material, is the insolvency of a debtor at the date of the balance sheet which only became known after that date but before the financial statements were approved by the board of directors.

CONSOLIDATED INCOME STATEMENT

The second important financial statement is the consolidated income statement (also known as the consolidated profit and loss account). While a balance sheet presents the financial position of a company at a point in time, an income statement relates to a period, for example the year ended 31 December 2005. It shows, from the point of view of the shareholders, the results of the year's activities.

The key items in BPI's 2005 consolidated income statement are as follows:

	£m
Turnover (i.e. sales)	410.2
Profit from operations	23.3
Profit before tax	19.7
Profit for the year	14.3

The format of consolidated income statements is more variable than that of consolidated balance sheets and thus harder to explain. Essentially, however, all UK income statements can be viewed as a series of significant sub-totals. The first item in the income statement is turnover or sales. This represents the net amounts invoiced to external customers by companies in the group but excludes rebates, discounts, value added taxes and other sales-related taxes. It also excludes the sales of associates and sales within the group between the parent and its subsidiaries. An analysis of turnover by class of business and by geographical origin is given in the notes (segment information is discussed in Chapter 6).

Cost of sales (the cost of goods sold during the accounting period whether manufactured during the period or not) is deducted from turnover to give gross profit. From this, in the BPI income statement, are further deducted distribution costs, selling and administrative expenses, and the amount applied to the employee profit-sharing scheme, to give profit from operations. Other companies use different classifications of costs and expenses. Companies typically do not disclose the detail of all the items that are deducted from gross profit to arrive at profit from operations but disclose in the notes significant items such as staff costs (wages and salaries, and social security and pensions), depreciation and amortization, operating lease charges (see Chapter 8), and auditors' remuneration (see Chapter 3).

The main item to be added or subtracted from profit from operations to arrive at earnings (profit) before interest (EBIT) is the group share of the profits and losses of associates. The accounting treatment of associates differs, as we have seen above, from that of subsidiaries. Like the latter, the appropriate share of profit or loss before tax, not just dividends receivable, is brought into the group results. Unlike the latter, it is brought in as one figure, not split into its component parts. This is because the group controls the turnover, wages and salaries of its subsidiaries but not of its associates.

After EBIT the next significant sub-total is profit before tax. This is net of financing costs. The financing costs include not only interest paid on loans and other borrowings but also interest on pension liabilities net of the expected return on pension scheme assets. Subtracting the tax charge for the year from the profit before tax produces the profit after tax. This is divided between the shareholders of the parent company (£14.2m in the case of BPI in 2005) and the minority interests (£0.1m).

At the foot of the consolidated income statement a note is given of the earnings per share (EPS). EPS is based on earnings per *ordinary* share. The relevant figure for earnings is net of all expenses and amounts due to other shareholders, including preference shareholders and minority shareholders. Thus for BPI in 2005 it was £14.2m. EPS is not of interest to preference shareholders since their dividend is fixed irrespective of the level of earnings. As at 31 December 2005, BPI had issued 25,894,393 ordinary shares. Since, however, earnings are a measure over a period, the EPS calculation is based not on the number of shares at the end of the period but on the weighted average of ordinary shares in issue during the year. The weighted average is the number of shares at the beginning of the period, adjusted by the number of shares issued and repurchased during the period weighted by the dates of issue and repurchase. The weighted average for BPI in 2005 was (to the nearest 1,000) 25,726,000 shares, so the calculation of 'basic' EPS was:

$$\text{EPS} = \frac{14,200,000 \times 100\text{p}}{25,726,000} = 55.20\text{p}.$$

The concept of earnings per share, and in particular 'diluted' EPS, is discussed further in Chapter 8.

Profit earned needs to be related to investment made. Profitability and return on investment form the main subjects of Chapter 6.

STATEMENT OF RECOGNIZED INCOME AND EXPENSE / STATEMENT OF CHANGES IN EQUITY

Not all items of income and expense are passed through the income statement. Those that are not are disclosed either in a consolidated statement of recognized income and expense (SORIE) (as published by most UK listed companies) or in a statement of changes in equity. The difference between the SORIE and the statement of changes in equity is that the latter (but not the former) shows dividends and other transactions between the company and its shareholders. The inclusion of these transactions provides a clearer link between the balance sheet and the income statement but it blurs the distinction between capital movements and income movements. A logical starting point for such statements is the profit for the year after tax, taken from the foot of the income statement, but some companies use other presentations. The items disclosed include actuarial gains and losses on defined benefit pension schemes, foreign currency translation differences (discussed later in this chapter), and some changes in fair values. After adding and subtracting these items from the profit after tax of £14.2m, BPI's total recognized income and expense for 2005 amounted to £6.5m, all but £0.1m of which was attributable to the shareholders of the parent company.

CASH FLOW STATEMENT

Neither the balance sheet nor the income statement directly discloses the inflows and outflows of cash into a group of companies during a financial year. This is provided by the consolidated cash flow statement. An important figure in this statement is cash generated from operations. Since, as will be stressed in Chapter 7, increasing cash and making profits are not the same, this figure may differ considerably from profit before tax. For example, in 2005 the BPI group generated cash of £33.8m from operations, compared with profit before tax of £19.7m. The cash flow statement provides a reconciliation between the two figures. The main reasons for the difference are that depreciation and amortization do not involve cash outflows and that profit calculations are based on movements in all components of working capital, not just cash. Adjustments must therefore be made for changes in inventories and in accounts receivable and payable. This might be thought to be a rather roundabout way of calculating the cash generated. It is in fact known as the 'indirect method'. The 'direct method' is easier to understand since it simply lists the cash receipts and payments under each heading. However, it lacks a link to the income statement and is more difficult to prepare for a group of companies. Most groups use the indirect method.

Deduction of net interest and tax paid provides a figure for net cash from operating activities (£26.6m for BPI in 2005). This figure is sometimes referred to as free cash flow, since it can be used at the discretion of the directors either for investment or for paying dividends to the equity shareholders. Investment can of course also be financed by borrowing. Note that net interest and tax *paid* differ from the interest and tax figures in the income statement, which take account of amounts owing at the beginning and end of the financial year.

Having established net cash from operations, the cash flow statement moves on to show cash from investing activities and financing activities. BPI invested £11.6m in 2005 in net purchases of property, plant and equipment and intangible assets. Its net cash flows for the year before any financing activities was therefore £26.6m − £11.6m = £15.0m. Its financing activities included repaying loans, issuing and repurchasing shares, and paying dividends, amounting in total to minus £7.7m. Its net increase in cash and cash equivalents during the year was therefore £15.0m − £7.7m = £7.3m. This figure added to that for cash and cash equivalents at the beginning of the period (minus £12.4m) gives (after an adjustment of £0.2m for the effect of changes in foreign exchange rates) cash and cash equivalents at the end of the year of minus £4.9m. A successful year enabled BPI both to increase dividends to shareholders and to reduce its bank overdraft.

FOREIGN EXCHANGE

Subsidiaries and associates outside the UK normally keep their accounts and prepare their financial statements in the local currency of the country in which they operate. This is termed the 'functional currency'. For example, the functional currency of the US subsidiary of a UK parent will be dollars, whereas the 'reporting currency' of the group in its annual report will be sterling. Table 2.1 shows the fluctuation of the pound sterling since 1999 against two widely used currencies, the US dollar and the euro. The size of the fluctuations suggests that the choice of a method to translate dollars, euros, etc. into sterling could have a significant effect on the figures in the consolidated statements of the many British companies who operate overseas.

The 'closing rate' method is used for subsidiaries and associates which operate as separate or quasi-independent entities and in which the parent company is deemed to have a 'net investment' rather than an investment in each individual asset and liability. Under this method, assets and liabilities are translated at year-end rates and items in the profit and loss account are translated at average rates. Any differences on translation which arise from changing exchange rates are passed not through the consolidated income statement but through the statement of recognized income and expense or the statement of changes in equity, and thus do not affect reported profits.

The closing rate method is not used when subsidiaries are deemed not to be independent of the parent company. In this case, the 'temporal method' is used instead. This differs from the closing rate method in that those assets (mostly property, plant and equipment and inventories) which are recorded in the local currency at historical cost rather than at current value are translated at the rates ruling at the dates at which they were acquired by the subsidiary. Also, and very importantly, exchange gains and losses are passed through the income statement. Under the temporal method, groups whose parent company's currency is strengthening tend to show translation gains, while those whose parent company's currency is weakening tend to show translation losses. For foreign subsidiaries in economies experiencing very high rates of inflation ('hyperinflation'), the unadjusted closing rate method will give misleading results unless the local currency is first adjusted for inflation.

Foreign exchange *transactions* are translated into sterling at the rate of exchange at the date of the transactions or at the appropriate forward contract rate.

Table 2.1 The rate of exchange of £1 sterling to US$1 and €1, 1999–2006

	$	Euro
31 December 1999	1.62	1.61
2000	1.49	1.60
2001	1.46	1.64
2002	1.61	1.54
2003	1.78	1.42
2004	1.93	1.41
2005	1.72	1.47
2006	1.96	1.49

Source UN Monthly Bulletin of Statistics

SUMMARY FINANCIAL STATEMENTS

The cost of sending out a full set of financial statements is quite considerable, especially for a company such as BG, which, as noted in Chapter 1, has over 800,000 shareholders. It is probably for this reason that listed companies are permitted to issue financial statements which summarize the information contained in the annual report. The issue of summary financial statements is optional (BPI, with far fewer shareholders than BG, does not issue them). Moreover, shareholders who state that they wish to receive the full financial statements must be sent them. The minimum form and content of financial statements is prescribed by regulation and comprise the main items from the directors' report, the consolidated income statement and consolidated balance sheet. Some companies (e.g. Tesco) publish more than this and may also take the opportunity to include 'glossy' annual review material. In this form, these documents often have longer print runs than the full version of the annual report. A summary financial statement is not the same as a simplified statement. It is less intimidating in bulk but not necessarily easier to understand.

3

Taxation and Audit

> Taxation?
> Wherein? And what taxation? My Lord Cardinal,
> You that are blamed alike with us,
> Know you of this taxation?
> > William Shakespeare, *King Henry the Eighth,* I, ii

> Never ask of money spent
> Where the spender thinks it went
> Nobody was ever meant
> To remember or invent
> What he did with every cent
> > Robert Frost, 'The Hardship of Accounting'

This chapter deals briefly with two important matters of which all readers of company annual reports should have some knowledge: taxation and audit. No attempt will be made to cover either in detail. Company taxation in particular is a fearsomely complicated subject, with constantly changing rules.

TAXATION IN THE FINANCIAL STATEMENTS

The first point to note is that in the UK, the rules for computing taxable income are somewhat 'disconnected' from the rules for calculating accounting profit. In other words, companies have to comply with financial reporting standards (see Chapter 4) in their financial statements, not with taxation legislation. This does not mean that the two sets of rules do not influence each other, but there are important differences, as will be seen below. Nevertheless, and this is the second point, there are many items in financial statements that can only be understood with some knowledge of the tax system.

The places where references to taxation can be found in the financial statements can be illustrated from the 2005 statements of BPI. Tax on profit on ordinary activities is stated in the consolidated income statement to be £5.4 million, which is 27 per cent of the profit before tax of £19.7 million. Why was it not 30 per cent, given that that was the standard rate of corporation tax on profits in 2005? BPI's explanations in the notes illustrate the many ways in which the calculations of reported profit and taxable income can differ. Some expenses charged against profit are not tax deductible; the tax allowance for depreciation is different from that charged in the income statement; tax losses are utilized; part of the profit is subject to tax outside the UK; an adjustment is made in respect of prior years.

In the consolidated balance sheet, tax appears as a current liability and also, more mysteriously, as deferred taxation. Among BPI's current liabilities at 31 December 2005 is the sum of £3.8 million for current tax. This relates mainly to tax on the profits for 2005 not yet due to be paid. Tax actually paid in 2005 is shown in BPI's consolidated cash flow statement to be £4.0 million. Included under BPI's non-current assets and non-current liabilities at 31 December 2005 are deferred tax assets of £12.2 million and deferred tax liabilities of £2.3 million respectively. Deferred tax is *not* an amount of tax which HM Revenue and Customs has permitted the company to postpone. Rather, it is the recognition of the tax implied (but not otherwise included) by the figures in the financial statements. This is explained in more detail below.

Companies do not just pay tax; they also collect tax on behalf of the tax authorities. Income tax and national insurance are deducted under the pay as you earn (PAYE) system from employees' salaries and wages. At balance sheet date this gives rise to a current liability for amounts not yet passed on. The effect of value added tax (VAT) on figures in the financial statements is explained below.

CORPORATION TAX AND TAX CREDITS

British companies pay corporation tax not income tax. Taxable income is measured in much the same way as accounting profit, but with many exceptions, the major one being depreciation. The corporation tax rate is usually set annually in arrears for the tax year 1 April to 31 March. The tax is *assessed*, however, on the basis of a company's accounting period, which may end on a different date, such as 31 December. The rate of corporation tax can vary. In the financial year 2006 (i.e. from 1 April 2006 to 31 March 2007) it was 30 per cent. The lower rate of 19 per cent applied to companies with small profits.

Shareholders are assessed to income tax on the basis of the dividends they receive, grossed up by a tax credit, but can set the tax credit against their liability to income tax. The example below, which assumes a corporation tax rate of 30 per cent and a starting rate of income tax of 10 per cent (the rates in force when this chapter was written), shows how this 'imputation system', as it is called, works from the point of view of the shareholder.

Suppose, in the example, that the shareholder is a woman, not a company, who holds 1 per cent of the shares of a company. She would be assessed for income tax on £48,890 not £44,000, but the tax credit would be offset against the tax payable. The amount of the tax credit is not recorded in the company's financial statements.

	£000
Taxable profit (assumed to be equal to the accounting profit)	10,000
Corporation tax at 30%	3,000
Profit after tax	7,000
Dividend paid	4,400
Retained profit	2,600

The shareholders receive:

	£m
Dividend	4,400
plus Tax credit (10/90 × £4,400,000)	489
	4,889

CAPITAL ALLOWANCES AND INVESTMENT INCENTIVES

As already noted in Chapter 2, the tax deductions allowed for the wear and tear on assets (known as 'capital allowances') differ in amount from the depreciation recorded in a company's accounts. The main reason for this is that whereas a company in reporting to its shareholders is required by financial reporting standards to calculate profit as fairly as possible, the government may also be interested in trying to encourage investment. The method of calculating capital allowances has varied from time to time, as have the rates allowed. The rates vary according to the class of asset. At the time of writing the main rates were 25 per cent on plant and machinery, and 4 per cent on industrial buildings. There are no capital allowances on non-industrial buildings such as retail shops and office buildings.

All the allowances described above operate as deductions in the calculation of taxable income. A company which has no taxable income to offset against the allowances does not benefit. This is not true of government grants. These are not reductions in taxable income but payments of cash by the government to the company. They are thus not dependent on the company making a taxable profit. Companies credit grants related to property, plant and equipment to income over the estimated useful life of the asset. The balance of the grant is usually carried forward in the balance sheet as a deferred credit. The depreciation charged is calculated on the cost of the asset gross of the grant. An alternative permissible treatment, which produces a different balance sheet but has the same net effect on the income statement, is to record the cost of the asset as net of the grant, record no income from the grant, and calculate depreciation on the net cost.

DEFERRED TAXATION

Capital allowances greater than accounting depreciation ('accelerated capital allowances') are an example of what are known as 'temporary differences'. The effect in this case is to show the asset in the balance sheet at a higher amount than in the tax records, and to reduce taxable income in the current year below the company's profit before tax. It is standard accounting practice, nevertheless, to base the taxation charge in the income statement not on the tax records but on the figures in the financial statements. The argument is that the taxation payable has not been saved but merely deferred to a later year, and that therefore the tax charge in the income statement should be based on the accounting values and a liability to pay the deferred tax should be recognized in the balance sheet. In other cases the effect may work in the other direction and give rise to a deferred taxation asset. How much tax has been deferred and how and when to recognize it has been debated at length. The current consensus is that the balance sheet liability method should be used. Deferred tax liabilities are recognized for all taxable temporary differences and deferred tax assets are recognized to the extent that it is probable that taxable profits will be available against which deductible temporary differences can be utilized. The carrying amount of deferred tax assets is reviewed at each balance sheet date and reduced to the extent that it is no longer probable that sufficient taxable profits will be available to allow all or part of the asset to be recovered. Deferred tax is calculated at the tax rates that are expected to apply in the period when the liability is settled or the asset is realized. Deferred tax is charged or credited in the income statement, except when it relates to items charged or credited directly to equity, in which case the deferred tax is also dealt with in equity.

It is important to note that companies are required to take a balance sheet rather than an income statement approach (see Chapter 2). This has several consequences. First, deferred tax is recognized not just on operating profits but also on gains (which may be taxable if realized) recorded on the revaluation of assets such as land and buildings. Second, the rate of tax assumed on the deferred taxable amount is that appropriate when the tax will be payable, not that at the date the profit or gain was first recognized. In practice, of course, rates of tax are not known very far into the future, so rates at the date of the balance sheet are used, and changed if necessary from year to year. Third, deferred taxation can be an asset if accounting profits are lower than taxable income. However, like any other assets, deferred taxation assets are only recognized when probable, i.e. if there is a reasonable probability that there will be taxable profits in the future to allow them to be recovered. In 2005 the deferred tax assets of BPI and many other companies were greater than their deferred tax liabilities. The main reason for this was that many companies record in their income statements a much larger charge for employee benefits than is allowed for tax purposes. Accounting for employee retirement benefits was discussed in Chapter 2.

The calculations for deferred taxation can be difficult to understand and the standards have changed several times. Not surprisingly, perhaps, research provides little evidence that deferred taxation numbers are value relevant or provide other useful information.

CAPITAL GAINS TAX

Individuals are taxed not only on their income but also on certain capital gains; that is, the excess of the price they receive on selling an asset over the price they paid for it. They are entitled to an annual exempt amount on which tax is not payable. Companies are also taxed on their capital gains, which are charged to corporation tax. Tax does not become payable when an asset is revalued but only when it is sold, and even then the tax payable is postponed if a replacement is bought. However, as noted above, there may nevertheless be a deferred tax charge in the financial statements.

VALUE ADDED TAX

Unlike the forms of taxation discussed so far, value added tax (VAT) is an indirect tax not a direct tax; that is, one that is not assessed and collected from those intended to bear it (the final consumers). VAT is a multi-stage tax: manufacturing companies such as BPI pay tax on their inputs and can set off the tax paid against the tax charged. Sales and purchases are included in the income statement net of VAT, but trade receivables (debtors) and payables (creditors) in the balance sheet include VAT.

TAX LAW

The most important statutes (Acts of Parliament) relating to the taxes described in this chapter are the Income and Corporation Taxes Act 1988, the Capital Allowances Act 1990, the Taxation of Chargeable Gains Act 1992, and the Taxes Management Act 1970. Every year there is at least one Finance Act amending the law. There is also a large body of case law relating to taxation. Tax practitioners cope by subscribing to multi-volume tax guides (available both in hard copy and in electronic form) which are constantly updated.

AUDIT REPORTS

The best way to explain what constitutes an audit in the UK is to analyse a typical audit report on the consolidated financial statements of a listed company, as set out below:

Independent Auditors' Report to the Members of XYZ PLC
We have audited the group and parent financial statements ['the financial statements'] of XYZ PLC for the year ended 31 December 20xx which comprise the group income statement, the group and parent company balance sheets, the group cash flow statement, the group statement of recognized income and expense and the related notes. These financial statements have been prepared under the accounting policies set out therein. We have also audited the information in the Directors' Remuneration Report that is described as being audited.

The report is made solely to the company's members, as a body, in accordance with section 495 of the Companies Act 2006. Our audit work has been undertaken so that we might state to the company's members those matters that we are required to state to them in an audit report and for no other purpose. To the fullest extent permitted by law, we do not accept or assume responsibility to any one other than the company and the company's members as a body, for our audit work, for this report, or for the opinions we have formed.

Respective Responsibilities of Directors and Auditors
The directors' responsibilities for preparing the directors' report and the group financial statements in accordance with applicable law and International Financial

Reporting Standards (IFRS) as adopted by the EU, and for preparing the company financial statements and the Directors' Remuneration Report in accordance with applicable law and UK Accounting Standards (UK Generally Accepted Accounting Practice) are set out in the Statement of Directors' Responsibilities.

Our responsibility is to audit the financial statements in accordance with relevant legal and regulatory requirements and International Standards on Auditing (UK and Ireland).

We report to you our opinion as to whether the financial statements give a true and fair view and whether the financial statements and the part of the Directors' Remuneration Report to be audited have been properly prepared in accordance with the Companies Act 2006 and whether, in addition, the group financial statements have been properly prepared in accordance with Article 4 of the IAS Regulation. We also report to you if, in our opinion, the directors' report is not consistent with the financial statements, if the company has not kept proper accounting records, if we have not received all the information and explanations we require for our audit or if information specified by law regarding directors' remuneration and other transactions is not disclosed.

We review whether the Corporate Governance Statement reflects the company's compliance with the nine provisions of the 2006 FRC Combined Code specified for our review by the Listing Rules of the Financial Services Authority, and we report if it does not. We are not required to consider whether the board's statements on internal control cover all risks and controls, or form an opinion on the effectiveness of the group's corporate governance procedures or its risk and control procedures.

We read the other information, including the directors' report, contained in the annual report and consider whether it is consistent with the audited group financial statements. We consider the implications for our report if we become aware of any apparent misstatements or material inconsistencies with the group financial statements. Our responsibilities do not extend to any other information.

Basis of audit opinion
We conducted our audit on the basis of International Standards on Auditing (UK and Ireland) issued by the Auditing Practices Board. An audit includes examination, on a test basis, of evidence relevant to the amounts and disclosures in the financial statements. It also includes an assessment of the significant estimates and judgements made by the directors in the preparation of the financial statements and of whether the accounting policies are appropriate to the group's and company's circumstances, consistently applied and adequately disclosed.

We planned and performed our audit so as to obtain all the information and explanations which we considered necessary in order to provide us with sufficient evidence to give reasonable assurance that the financial statements and the part of the Directors' Remuneration Report to be audited are free from material misstatement whether caused by fraud or other irregularity or error. In forming our opinion we also evaluated the overall adequacy of the presentation of information in the financial statements and the part of the Directors' Remuneration Report to be audited.

Opinion

In our opinion:

● The group financial statements give a true and fair view, in accordance with IFRS as adopted by the EU, of the state of the group's affairs as at 31 December 20xx and of its profit for the year then ended;

● The group financial statements have been properly prepared in accordance with the Companies Act 2006 and Article 4 of the IAS Regulation;

● The parent company financial statements give a true and fair view, in accordance with UK Generally Accepted Accounting Practice, of the state of the parent company's financial affairs as at 31 December 20xx;

● The parent company's financial statements have been properly prepared in accordance with the Companies Act 2006; and

● The parts of the Directors' Remuneration Report to be audited have been properly prepared in accordance with the Companies Act 2006.

XXXX
Chartered Accountants
Registered Auditors
Address
Date

The audit of large listed companies in the UK is dominated by only four firms. These are the 'Big Four' international accountancy firms: Deloitte, Ernst & Young, KPMG and PricewaterhouseCoopers. For example, of the companies referred to in this book, BP was audited in 2005 by Ernst & Young, BPI by KPMG, Centrica by Pricewaterhouse-Coopers and Vodaphone by Deloitte. In 2006, all but one of the FTSE 100 companies were audited by these firms. Their dominance is world-wide, not just in the UK, and is related to the emergence of multinational enterprises and the globalization of capital markets.

The audit report is signed by the senior statutory auditor (the partner in charge of the audit) for and on behalf of the audit firm. Auditors sign both as 'Chartered Accountants' and as 'Registered Auditors'. This dual description recognizes firstly that the firms' partners are members of a professional accountancy body and secondly, that the firm's name is inscribed on a statutory register as qualified for appointment as a company auditor. All three Institutes of Chartered Accountants (in England and Wales, of Scotland, and in Ireland) provide, as does the Association of Chartered Certified Accountants, a recognized professional qualification for company auditors, and maintain registers. Until recently, all audit firms were partnerships with unlimited liability. Most of the larger firms are now limited liability partnerships (LLPs: see Chapter 1); KPMG Audit is a plc.

There are many interesting points to note about the auditors' report:

1. It is lengthy and repetitive, mainly because of the auditors' aim (partly driven by fear of litigation) to set out clearly and unambiguously what they do and what they do not do. The auditors make a careful distinction between the respective responsibilities of the directors and the auditors.

2. The auditors are concerned in the report to limit their legal liability as far as possible. They do so in part by claiming that their report is intended only for the shareholders of the parent company and only as a body. This follows the much criticized Caparo case (1990), in which the House of Lords held that auditors owe a duty of care only to the shareholders as a body, not to individual shareholders or to other persons.

3. It is a report, not a certificate or a guarantee. The auditors report their opinion; they do not certify or guarantee anything.

4. What they give their opinion on is compliance with the Companies Act and the IAS Regulation of the EU, and on whether the financial statements give 'a' (not 'the') true and fair view. This is not the same as saying that the financial statements are 'correct' or 'right' in every particular. It should be clear from the discussion of the financial statements in Chapter 2 that figures in balance sheets, income statements and even cash flow statements are necessarily based to a certain extent on estimates and judgements made by the directors, and on particular sets of rules such as IFRS and UK GAAP. Note that these rules are not identical and that the application of either could result in 'a true and fair view'. Note also, that it is not a true and fair view

as such that is said to be given, but a true and fair view in accordance with a set of rules.

5. The auditors are reporting to the 'members' (i.e. the shareholders) of the parent company, not to the directors. Their function, as a late nineteenth-century English judge put it, is to serve as a 'watchdog' for the shareholders. They are appointed by the shareholders, usually on the recommendation of the directors. Appointment is made each year by resolution at the annual general meeting.

6. The auditors do not report on whether or not frauds have been committed, but limit themselves to stating that they have sought reasonable assurance that the financial statements are free of any material misstatements caused by fraud.

7. A brief description is given of the way in which the audit is carried out, with a reference to the UK and Irish version of international auditing standards issued by the Auditing Practices Board.

8. The audit of a large company will always include a consideration of the effectiveness of the company's system of internal control, but the auditors are careful to state the limits of the tests that they have performed on this. One reason is to make clear that they are not claiming to comply with the stringent rules of the US Sarbanes–Oxley Act.

The report set out above is suitable when the auditors give an unqualified opinion. Occasionally auditors give a qualified opinion or are even unable to form an opinion (known as 'disclaimer of opinion'). Qualified opinions may arise if there is a limitation on the scope of the auditors' examination or if the auditors are in disagreement with the directors on the treatment or disclosure of a matter in the financial statements.

AUDIT EXPECTATIONS GAP

The wording of audit reports is an amalgam of legal requirements and of what the audit profession considers to be the function of an audit. This does not necessarily coincide with what all users of audit reports would prefer and in recent decades there has been a recognition of what is known as the 'audit expectations gap'.

A discussion document 'Auditing into the Twenty-first Century' issued by the Research Committee of the Institute of Chartered Accountants of Scotland in 1993 identified these public expectations as follows.

1. The financial statements are right.
2. The company will not fail.
3. There has been no fraud.
4. The company has acted within the law.
5. The company has been competently managed.
6. The company has adopted a responsible attitude to environmental and social matters.
7. The external auditors are independent of the directors.
8. The external auditors will report to a third party if they suspect that the directors are involved in fraud or other illegal activity.
9. The external auditors are accountable to a wide range of stakeholders.
10. The external auditors are financially liable if they fail in any of their duties.

Some of these expectations are already being met in whole or in part, but neither the government nor the accountancy profession is likely to accept that all of them are reasonable, in the sense that there is an effective demand for them and that there are auditors (not necessarily the existing firms) capable of supplying them at a cost that someone is willing to pay.

We have already seen that no set of financial statements can be regarded as 'right' as distinct from 'true and fair'. Auditors are likely to continue to report on the latter. Neither the directors nor the auditors can guarantee that a company will not fail but directors could reasonably be expected to state, and auditors to report on, whether or not a company is likely to be a going concern for the ensuing twelve months. At present, a statement that the company is a going concern is usually made in the Operating and Financial Review (see Chapter 1). Auditors cannot guarantee that there has been no material fraud but they can report whether or not there are systems of internal control which minimize opportunities for fraud and maximize the likelihood that any such fraud will be quickly detected. At present, the directors report on internal control within their Corporate Governance statement (see Chapter 1). The auditors expressly state that they are not required to consider whether the board's statement on internal control covers all risks and controls. Moreover, auditors, as experts in accounting, are not necessarily qualified to assess the competence of management or to report on environmental or social matters. Some companies, BPI among them, publish corporate social responsibility reviews (see Chapter 1), but these are not a legal requirement and they are not audited.

It is obviously important that auditors should not only be skilled in their profession but also be, and be seen to be, independent of the directors and management of the company being audited. Company law requires that an auditor should not be an officer of the company, or of any company in the group, or a partner or employee of such an officer or servant. The amount of the auditors' remuneration must be disclosed in the annual report. Auditors may (and commonly do) also provide other services (e.g. taxation advice) to companies that they audit, although some commentators argue that this may compromise their independence. The amount received for any such services must be separately disclosed. BPI, for example, discloses audit fees of £200,000 in 2005 and a charge for tax services of the same amount. Most listed companies have established audit committees of non-executives. Their function is to review the annual and half-yearly financial statements and all matters related to both internal and external audit.

Auditors of financial institutions are required to report to a regulatory body when they are satisfied that it is necessary to do so in order to protect the interests of shareholders or depositors. It is possible that, despite the problems of confidentiality, this obligation may be extended to other types of companies.

As already noted, the report of the external auditors is in practice relied upon by many other stakeholders than the shareholders, but audit firms, fearful of litigation, have strongly resisted any extension of their liability. The Companies Act 2006 permits companies and auditors to enter into liability limitation agreements that limit the auditors' liability to what is fair and reasonable.

SUPERVISION OF AUDITORS

Who shall audit the auditors? Formal supervision of auditors in the UK began with the implementation of the EU Eighth Directive in the Companies Act 1989. It was this Act that brought in the requirement that company auditors must be registered auditors, i.e. have their names inscribed as qualified for appointment on a statutory register maintained by recognized supervisory bodies. This legislation meant that the professional bodies had to supervise their members in the public interest, whilst at the same time continuing to serve the private interests of their members. This combination of roles can lead to a conflict of interest, and, combined with the impact of auditing scandals in the US and continental Europe which cast doubt on auditor independence, led eventually to the setting up of a Professional Oversight Board (POB) responsible to the Financial Reporting Council (see Chapter 4). POB is independent of the accountancy profession and accountancy firms. Its responsibilities include overseeing the regulation of auditors by the recognized supervisory bodies, monitoring the quality of the audits of economically significant entities, and overseeing the regulation of the accountancy profession by the professional accountancy bodies. It has set up an Audit Inspection Unit. Auditors are also influenced by the Financial Reporting Review Panel (see Chapter 4).

4

Accounting Regulation and Accounting Concepts

ACCOUNTING REGULATION

It is clear from the preceding chapters that the preparers of company financial statements in the UK are following complicated and detailed sets of rules. These rules may appear to be highly technical, and indeed they are. This might suggest that the formulation of the rules should be left to the experts, but experts in any field, as is well known, may disagree with each other and may be influenced by vested interests. At the same time, the interests of many stakeholders may be affected by the choices that the experts make, and if those rules are enforced, the stakeholders are likely to wish to influence the rules in their own favour. In this chapter we explain both who sets the rules (the 'standard-setters') for UK companies and who and what influences the content of the rules. We also discuss how the rules are enforced.

THE STANDARD-SETTERS

The rules for the consolidated statements of UK listed companies are set out in International Financial Reporting Standards (IFRS) as promulgated by the International Accounting Standards Board (IASB) and adopted by the European Union (EU). A list of the standards is given in Table 4.1. The IASB is a private-sector body with headquarters in London. The membership of its board currently comprises accountants not only from the EU (the UK, France, Germany and Sweden) but also from other countries such as Canada, Japan and the US (whose companies are not permitted to use IFRS), and from Australia and South Africa.

Table 4.1 IASB Standards Extant mid 2007

IAS	1	Presentation of financial statements
IAS	2	Inventories
IAS	7	Cash flow statements
IAS	8	Accounting policies, changes in accounting estimates and errors
IAS	10	Events after the balance sheet date
IAS	11	Construction contracts
IAS	12	Income taxes
IAS	16	Property, plant and equipment
IAS	17	Leases
IAS	18	Revenue
IAS	19	Employee benefits
IAS	20	Accounting for government grants and disclosure of government assistance
IAS	21	The effects of changes in foreign exchange rates
IAS	23	Borrowing costs
IAS	24	Related party disclosures
IAS	26	Accounting and reporting by retirement benefit plans
IAS	27	Consolidated and separate financial statements
IAS	28	Investments in associates
IAS	29	Financial reporting in hyperinflationary economies
IAS	30	Disclosure in the financial statements of banks
IAS	31	Interests in joint ventures
IAS	32	Financial instruments: presentation
IAS	33	Earnings per share
IAS	34	Interim financial reporting
IAS	36	Impairment of assets
IAS	37	Provisions, contingent liabilities and contingent assets
IAS	38	Intangible assets
IAS	39	Financial instruments: recognition and measurement
IAS	40	Investment property
IAS	41	Agriculture
IFRS	1	First-time adoption of international financial reporting standards
IFRS	2	Share-based payment
IFRS	3	Business combinations

IFRS	4	Insurance contracts
IFRS	5	Non-current assets held for sale and discontinued operations
IFRS	6	Exploration for and evaluation of mineral resources
IFRS	7	Financial instruments: disclosures
IFRS	8	Operating segments

For all other UK company financial statements, including the individual statements of the listed parent company, the preparers must follow *either* IFRS *or* the Financial Reporting Standards (FRS) of the UK Accounting Standards Board (ASB). The latter constitute what is known as UK GAAP (in contrast to US GAAP and International GAAP). GAAP is here an acronym for Generally Accepted Accounting Practice. It was first used in the US, where it meant, and still means, Generally Accepted Accounting Principles. To understand how this complicated situation came about it is necessary to provide some historical background.

The influence of accountants on the regulation of financial reporting in the UK is of long standing. The accountancy profession first got involved in setting accounting rules during the Second World War. Between 1942 and 1969 the Institute of Chartered Accountants in England and Wales (ICAEW), the largest of the professional accountancy bodies, issued a series of non-mandatory Recommendations on Accounting Principles. In 1970 it responded to what were widely regarded as damaging examples of misleading financial statements and some sustained hostile criticism of the profession in the media, by setting up an Accounting Standards Steering Committee, later renamed the Accounting Standards Committee (ASC) and joined by the other five professional accountancy bodies. However, all the members of the ASC were part-time and its role was confined to developing Statements of Standard Accounting Practice (SSAPs), whose adoption and enforcement remained the responsibility of the six professional bodies. In 1988 the Report of the Dearing Committee accepted the criticism that arrangements closer to those operating in the United States were preferable, and in 1990 in ASC was replaced by an Accounting Standards Board (ASB), independent of the professional bodies but still comprising mainly accountants. It currently has a full-time paid chairman, a full-time paid technical director and eight part-time paid members. The ASB is supervised by a Financial Reporting Council (FRC), also independent of the profession. Unlike the ASC, the ASB was given the power in the

Companies Act to issue accounting standards on its own authority. The ASB issues its own Financial Reporting Standards (FRS) and also adopted the extant SSAPs of the ASC, although many of these have now been superseded. Small companies and other entities need comply with only one standard: the Financial Reporting Standard for Smaller Entities (FRSSE). This is a recognition that the costs for small companies of complying with financial reporting standards may exceed the benefits to interested parties. FRSSE provides a useful summary of UK standards in many areas. There are thus effectively three sets of accounting standards for UK companies: IFRS, FRS and FRSSE. They are closely related to each other but by no means identical.

The setting of accounting standards by an international body began in 1973 when the International Accounting Standards Committee (IASC) was founded by the accountancy bodies of the UK and Ireland and eight other countries (Australia, Canada, France, Japan, Mexico, the Netherlands, the United States and West Germany). One of the driving forces behind its creation was the British accountant Sir Henry (later Lord) Benson. It is not coincidental that 1973 was also the year that the UK joined the Common Market (later the EU). Both UK and US accountants were concerned about the draft Fourth Directive (see Chapter 1), which contained unattractive accounting rules for UK companies and the continental European subsidiaries of multinationals. The IASC operated until 2001, when it was succeeded by the International Accounting Standards Board (IASB).

By the end of the 1990s, it was clear that the IASC was being more successful at harmonizing accounting rules than was the EU. In particular, many listed companies in the EU were (sometimes with the approval of their national governments, as in Germany) publishing consolidated statements based on international standards or on US GAAP. In the UK the ASB was issuing standards designed to be closely compatible with IFRS. In 2000, the EU Commission, which was keen to strengthen the EU capital markets by establishing a standardized accounting system, accepted the superiority of international standards by proposing that, from 2005, it should be compulsory for all listed companies in the EU to use IFRS for consolidated statements, thereby outlawing both domestic rules and US rules for this purpose. The Regulation was approved in 2002. However, the Commission does not wish to lose all control of accounting standards to an unelected private-sector body. New and revised IFRS cannot be endorsed in advance for EU use. An Accounting Regulatory Committee (ARC), comprising governmental representatives from all EU member states, considers whether changes to IFRS can be adopted in the EU. This means that EU-endorsed IFRS are not identical to IFRS proper. The European Financial Reporting Advisory Group (EFRAG), a private-sector committee of auditors, preparers and other experts, advises the ARC on new or amended IFRS. Most of the content of IFRS was adopted as it stood by the EU in 2004, with the important exception of IAS 39 on financial instruments (see the section below on political lobbying). IFRS will continue to evolve over time, as new problems arise and as the consensus as to what is conceptually correct and 'politically' acceptable changes. However, continual change is confusing and costly. The IASB in recent years has tried to achieve what is called a 'stable platform' of standards.

The Regulation allows member states to extend the use of IFRS compulsorily or optionally to unlisted companies and to unconsolidated statements. The member states are not at all consistent in this area. In the UK, the government has granted unlisted companies and listed companies in their non-consolidated statements the option of using either IFRS as adopted by the EU or UK standards as promulgated by the ASB. The ASB itself has decided to converge its standards with IFRS, i.e. to make them as similar to IFRS as is possible within the constraints of UK law. This has the obvious advantage of avoiding two conflicting sets of rules, but it does mean that sometimes the rules are not those which UK accountants and standard-setters might have chosen. In practice progress towards convergence has been slow.

Why have British governments and accounting standard-setters been willing to give up national setting of accounting standards for the consolidated financial statements of listed companies? There are several reasons. First, IFRS, although different from UK rules, are not so different as to be unacceptable. The content of IFRS has been much influenced by UK ideas and by UK accountants. Second, many UK companies operate and raise capital on a worldwide basis so it is in their interests and those of their auditors that there should be an internationally acceptable set of rules. Third, UK accountants would prefer that set of rules to be one whose content they can influence. The only alternative to IFRS is US GAAP whose content is determined by US domestic considerations. Fourth, the International Organization of Securities Commissions

(IOSCO), whose membership crucially includes the US Securities and Exchange Commission (SEC), has supported the idea of a set of international standards which would be accepted by all stock exchanges worldwide. This has not yet been achieved but efforts are being made to converge IFRS and US GAAP. Fifth, there are few tax complications, since, as explained in Chapter 3, in the UK tax accounting is for some topics 'disconnected' from reporting to shareholders. If HM Revenue and Customs do not like an IFRS rule, they can establish a different one for tax purposes. Sixth, companies are not prohibited from publishing internal accounting measures of performance or emphasizing what they regard as significant sub-totals, even if these are not consistent with IFRS. For example Centrica in 2005 contrasted its own preferred financial highlight measure of operating profit with what it termed statutory operating profit. The former was lower than the latter.

Although accountants, as technical experts, have been very influential in determining the content of IFRS and UK GAAP, other interested parties have also played a part. Particular financial reporting standards may have economic consequences that are of concern to governments and companies. Considered below are two aspects of the tension that sometimes exists between the technical experts and the 'politicians'. The former prefer standards that fit into their chosen conceptual framework. The latter may respond by political lobbying, i.e. by bringing pressure on standard-setters beyond a debate about the technical merits or the compliance costs of a proposed financial reporting standard.

CONCEPTUAL FRAMEWORK

The IASB's conceptual framework is contained in its *Framework for the Preparation and Presentation of Statements*. First published in 1989, it owes much to concepts developed mainly in the US from the 1970s onwards. It covers the objective of financial statements, the qualitative characteristics of financial information, the elements of financial statements, recognition in financial statements, and measurement in financial statements.

According to the *Framework*, the objective of financial statements is to provide to a wide range of users (present and potential investors, lenders, suppliers, employees, customers, governments and the public) information useful in making decisions about the financial position, performance and changes in financial position of an entity. Financial statements are general purpose, but the emphasis in the *Framework* is on investors in companies, who need to assess the stewardship of management and to make decisions about buying, selling and holding shares. Qualitative characteristics are those that make financial information useful. The most important are relevance, reliability, understandability and comparability. Financial statements should be understandable to those with a reasonable knowledge of business and accounting (obtained perhaps by studying a book such as this one). The statements should be comparable over time for the same entity and between entities. Ideally, information should be both relevant (have either predictive or confirmatory value and be material and timely) and reliable (provide a faithful representation, emphasize substance rather than form, be neutral, be prudent and be complete). In practice there may have to be a trade-off between these characteristics. For example, completely reliable information may be insufficiently timely to be relevant to action by users. A fair representation may sometimes be difficult to understand.

The elements of financial information are, as discussed in Chapter 2, assets, liabilities, equity, income and expense. The definitions given in that chapter follow those in the *Framework*. The existence of an asset or a liability does not necessarily mean that it should be 'recognized' in a financial statement; that is, depicted in both words and monetary amount and included in a statement total. Assets and liabilities are recognized only if there is evidence of a change in probable future economic benefits and the cost or value can be reliably measured. Recognition is usually triggered by a transaction but other events may also act as a trigger. Some events may, however, be difficult to measure reliably.

As we have seen in Chapter 2, a variety of measurement bases are used in financial statements, sometimes in combination with each other. The terminology can be confusing. Bases mentioned in the *Framework* are historical cost (the monetary amount for which an asset was originally purchased or produced), current replacement cost, net realizable value (the amount for which an asset can be sold, net of the expenses of completion and of sale) and present value (the value of the future net receipts, discounted to the present). Fair value (the amount at which an asset could be exchanged between a willing buyer and a willing seller) is referred to in several standards. These measurement bases have different degrees of relevance and reliability. Historical cost is the base most used, mainly because it is seen as being the most reliable. Its relevance can be doubted, however, for assets with volatile prices. Fair value may be more relevant in these cases, especially where market prices are readily available. Impairment losses are calculated with reference to recoverable amounts, defined as the higher of selling price and present value.

Conceptual frameworks set limits to rules but they do not rigidly confine them. Standards which are consistent with a conceptual framework but do not attempt to go into what is often inevitably arbitrary detail are said to be 'principles-based'; those which do go into such detail are said to be 'rules-based'. In practice this distinction may be a little blurred, but IFRS and UK GAAP are usually considered to be principles-based and US GAAP to be rules-based.

FORMATS

The IASB conceptual framework and IFRS pay little attention to the formats of financial statements. The formats chosen by the leading listed UK companies for their consolidated statements show the influence of traditional UK forms of presentation, the requirements of the Companies Act (largely derived in this context from the continental European-inspired directives of the EU) and the expectations of the international (especially the US) capital markets. The following generalizations can be made:

● The balance sheet is in a vertical, not two-sided form, starting with the least liquid assets (the non-current assets), followed by the current assets net of the current liabilities to give a figure of total assets less current liabilities that is equal to the sum of the non-current liabilities, shareholders' equity and minority interests that follow.
● The income statement is also vertical, starting with turnover (some-times called sales or revenue). The detailed expenses are shown not on the face of the income statement but in the notes, with disclosure of items such as employment costs and depreciation.

POLITICAL LOBBYING

However neutral and independent standard-setters try to be, their decisions may adversely affect the interests of companies and governments. These interested parties are likely to claim that the wording of a proposed standard that most suits them is the one with the greatest technical merit. If this fails to convince the standard-setter, they may resort to political lobbying. Two examples are share-based payments and financial instruments.

Share-based payments were discussed in Chapters 1 and 2 in the context of directors' remuneration. As a technical matter, almost all accountants agree that share-based payments, which include employee stock options, are part of employee compensation and should therefore be charged against income in each period in which the employee's services are performed, measured by the fair value of the options at the end of the period. This depresses the reported earnings of companies that prefer to pay their employees in this manner. In 2001 several European multinationals lobbied unsuccessfully against an IFRS mandating this treatment on the grounds that it would put them at a competitive disadvantage vis-à-vis US companies. In fact the US standard-setter agrees with the IASB on this matter but was prevented by political lobbying from implementing a standard until 2006.

Many continental European banks and politicians lobbied against the IASB's standard on financial instruments. The President of France even wrote in 2003 to the President of the European Commission on the subject. As a result, the Commission refused to adopt part of the financial instruments standard. The adopted version did not contain the option to 'mark to market' any financial liabilities (i.e. to value them at fair value and take the gains and losses to income) and allowed greater flexibility in the use of hedge accounting. However, in 2005, the IASB amended the standard, restricting the range of liabilities that can be fair valued. This was accepted by the Commission, so that the difference between the full standard and the EU-endorsed version concerns only hedge accounting.

CREATIVE ACCOUNTING

Financial statements can be used to mislead investors and other users as well as to inform them. Such 'creative accounting' became more common in the UK from the 1980s onwards. It can be easier to achieve where standards are rules-based rather than principles-based, often taking the form of creative compliance, whereby following the letter of a regulation is used to subvert its spirit. The overriding requirement to give a true and fair view ought to be able to prevent this, but it has not always succeeded in doing so in practice. The ASB and the IASB have had to work hard to combat the abuses of creative accounting. Some companies have exercised much ingenuity in 'managing' earnings (making them appear larger or less volatile than they really are), improving reported liquidity by 'window-dressing', and minimizing reported liabilities. There is a discussion of all of these in Chapters 6, 7 and 8.

MONITORING AND ENFORCEMENT

When the ASB was established in 1990 it was not given the role of monitoring or enforcing standards. Instead a separate Financial Reporting Review Panel (FRRP) was set up to monitor the financial statements of public and large private companies. Like the ASB, the FRRP was established as a subsidiary of a Financial Reporting Council (FRC), independent of both the profession and the government. The Panel played an important role in examining the financial statements of large companies for material departures from the Act and from financial reporting standards. It did not attempt to monitor all companies within its remit and did not attempt to be proactive, but restricted its investigations to companies brought to its attention. It achieved its aims by persuasion, although it had the power to apply to the court for a declaration that the financial statements of a company did not comply with the requirements of the Act (including giving a true and fair view) and for an order requiring the company's directors to prepare (and personally pay for) revised statements. The Panel established itself as an effective regulator, concerned to establish its legitimacy, despite its limited powers.

When the Financial Services Authority (FSA) was established in 2000 to regulate the financial services industry, it was given no part in enforcing compliance with financial reporting standards.

The role of the Panel was, however, re-considered in the light of the Enron case in the US and other accounting scandals. It was asked by the government to become more proactive and to explore ways of working with the FSA. From 2005 onwards one of the main tasks of the Panel has been to ensure compliance by listed companies with IFRS. The Panel currently selects financial statements for review both proactively and reactively. It discusses with the FSA and its own Standing Advisory Group which sectors of the economy are under strain or likely to give rise to difficult accounting issues. A number of financial statements are reviewed in the sectors thus selected. The Panel is developing a risk model to identify cases where accounting problems are more likely, e.g. where corporate governance is poor. It looks at topical accounting issues, and responds to complaints from the public, from the press and from the City of London. All selections take account of the risk of non-compliance and the risk of significant consequences in the event of non-compliance.

The Panel does not operate a system of advance clearance. It usually makes an announcement at the conclusion of an inquiry where the directors of the company under review have agreed that the financial statements under review were defective and required to be corrected or clarified. No announcement is usually made when financial statements are found not to be defective, although the Panel may, without naming companies, issue 'generic' press notices about matters that have come to its attention. The FRRP collaborates closely with the FSA. HM Revenue and Customs are authorized to disclose information regarding company accounts to the Panel.

Tools of Analysis and Useful Websites

... high Heaven rejects the lore
Of nicely-calculated less or more.

> William Wordsworth, 'Inside of King's College Chapel,
> Cambridge'

The first four chapters of this book have been mainly descriptive and explanatory. In the chapters that follow we turn to analysis and interpretation. We shall be concerned with three main questions:

1. Is the company under analysis making a satisfactory profit?
2. Is the company likely to run out of cash, or keep cash idle?
3. How does the company decide its long-term sources of funds?

These are the interrelated problems of profitability, liquidity and capital structure. Our tools of analysis are the relationships which exist among the different items in the financial statements ('financial ratios') and the rates of return linking outflows with expected inflows ('yields').

FINANCIAL RATIOS

Financial ratios are usually expressed either as percentages or as the number of times one figure can be divided into another. For example, if a company has current assets of £10 million and current liabilities of £5 million, we could say that current liabilities are 50% of current assets, that current assets are 200% of current liabilities, that the ratio

$$\frac{\text{current assets}}{\text{current liabilities}} \text{ is 2.0, or that the ratio } \frac{\text{current liabilities}}{\text{current assets}} \text{ is 0.5.}$$

Which method is chosen is a matter of convenience and convention. In the example quoted it is customary to speak of a current ratio, $\frac{\text{currents assets}}{\text{current liabilities}}$ of 2.0. A percentage, as can be seen from the above, is merely a ratio multiplied by 100.

Not all ratios and percentages are significant or useful, and one must guard against the temptation to calculate them for their own sake. The component parts of a ratio must be reasonably related to each other and measure something important. It is unlikely, for example, that much can be gained from a scrutiny of the relationship between current liabilities and goodwill. Accounting figures should not be treated as more precise than they really are; there is little sense in calculating a ratio to more than two decimal places. A single ratio in isolation seldom provides much information. Each ratio calculated should either provide additional information or act as a guide to the further questions which need to be asked.

YIELDS

A yield is a rate of return linking outflows to inflows. If for example I buy for £500 an irredeemable government bond with a par value of £1,000 on which interest of 4 per cent is payable annually, there is an immediate cash outflow of £500, followed by a series of cash inflows of £40 each year in perpetuity. The yield (before any tax) is $\frac{40 \times 100}{500}$ per cent (i.e. 8 per cent). If the bond were redeemable at a fixed price at some date in the future, there would be a difference between the flat yield, which takes only the interest into account, and the redemption yield which takes the redemption price into account as well. For example, if the bond is redeemable twenty years hence at par, the flat yield is about 5 per cent and the redemption yield is about 9.8 per cent.

THE NEED FOR COMPARISONS

As already noted, any ratio, percentage or yield is of little value in isolation. It is necessary to have some benchmark with which to compare it. The standard can be a budgeted one, set by the company for itself; a historical one, based on the past performance of the company; or an industry one, based on the observed ratios of companies in the same industry.

Budgeted standards are not usually available to shareholders or external financial analysts. Historical comparisons are often given in annual reports. For example, Johnson Matthey in its 2006 report provides a ten-year record of key income statement and balance sheet items, earnings per share and dividends per share.

INDUSTRY RATIOS

Industry average ratios pose a more difficult problem to the financial analyst. It is often difficult to decide to which industry a company belongs. Most financial analysts opt to use the industrial classification of the London Stock Exchange rather than the standard industrial classification (SIC) of economic activities used in government publications. Many industries are composed of a surprisingly heterogeneous group of companies. An extreme example in the Stock Exchange industrial classification is 'general industrials', of which BPI is a member. Johnson Matthey is in the 'chemicals' group and the 'speciality chemicals' sub-group. Another difficulty is that companies end their accounting periods on different dates (although 31 December and 31 March are the most popular) so that industry ratios are perforce averages of ratios calculated at different dates and for different periods. Care should therefore be taken when making industry comparisons based on ratios obtained from published financial statements.

USEFUL WEBSITES

The information in this book can be backed up, extended and updated through the use of the many websites maintained by UK government departments and agencies; UK, EU and international independent regulatory, standard-setting and advisory bodies; stock exchanges and stock exchange regulators; the Big Four accountancy firms; UK and Irish accountancy bodies; companies whose annual reports have been referred to in this book; annual report services; and commercial databases. A selection is given below.

UK GOVERNMENT DEPARTMENTS AND AGENCIES

The most useful websites under this heading are:

Department of Business, Enterprise and Regulatory Reform (DBERR)	www.dberr.gov.uk
Registrar of Companies (Companies House)	www.companieshouse.gov.uk
Financial Services Authority (FSA)	www.fsa.gov.uk
UK Listing Authority (UKLA)	www.fsa.gov.uk/ukla

All these government organizations have responsibilities that go well beyond the subject matter of the present book. From our point of view, the DBERR is important as the government department responsible for the reform of company legislation. Much of the administration of company law is carried out by Companies House, which is an executive agency of the DBERR. Companies House holds a mass of data relating to UK companies and limited partnerships. The FSA supervises the securities markets; the UKLA is the source of the listing requirements.

UK, EU AND INTERNATIONAL INDEPENDENT REGULATORY, STANDARD-SETTING AND ADVISORY BODIES

Accounting Standards Board (ASB) (UK)	www.frc.org.uk/asb
Auditing Practices Board (APB) (UK)	www.frc.org.uk/apb
European Financial Reporting Advisory Group (EFRAG)	www.efrag.org

Financial Reporting Council (FRC) (UK)	www.frc.org.uk
Financial Reporting Review Panel (FRRP) (UK)	www.frc.org.uk/frrp
International Accounting Standards Board (IASB)	www.iasb.org.uk
International Auditing and Assurances Standards Board (IAASB)	www.ifac.org/IAASB
Professional Oversight Board = (POB) (UK)	www.frc.org/pob

All these bodies have responsibilities relating to financial reporting, accounting and auditing which directly affect listed companies in the UK. Their origins and activities have been discussed in Chapters 3 and 4.

STOCK EXCHANGES AND STOCK EXCHANGE REGULATORS

Committee of European Securities Regulators (CESR)	www.cesr-eu.org
International Organization of Securities Commissions (IOSCO)	www.iosco.org
London Stock Exchange	www.londonstockexchange.com
Securities and Exchange Commission (SEC) (US)	www.sec.gov
World Federation of Exchanges	www.world-exchanges.org

BIG FOUR ACCOUNTANCY FIRMS (IFRS)

Deloitte	www.iasplus.com
Ernst & Young	www.ey.com
KPMG	www.kpmg.com
PricewaterhouseCoopers	www.pwc.com/ifrs

All the Big Four firms (and many other audit firms) provide useful information about IFRS on their websites. The iasplus site is especially recommended.

UK AND IRISH ACCOUNTANCY BODIES

Association of Chartered Certified Accountants (ACCA)	www.accaglobal.com
Chartered Institute of Management Accountants (CIMA)	www.cimaglobal.com
Chartered Institute of Public Finance and Accountancy (CIPFA)	www.cipfa.org.uk
Institute of Chartered Accountants in England and Wales (ICAEW)	www.icaew.co.uk
Institute of Chartered Accountants in Ireland (ICAI)	www.icai.ie
Institute of Chartered Accountants of Scotland (ICAS)	www.icas.org.uk

The ICAS and ICAEW websites are especially good sources of information on company financial reporting. The catalogue of the library of the ICAEW can be accessed online.

TAXATION

HM Revenue and Customs (HMRC)	www.hmrc.gov.uk
Institute for Fiscal Studies	www.ifs.org.uk

COMPANIES WHOSE ANNUAL REPORTS HAVE BEEN REFERRED TO IN THIS BOOK

BG	www.bg-group.com
BP	www.bp.com
British Polythene Industries	www.bpipoly.com
Cadbury Schweppes	www.cadburyschweppes.com
Centrica	www.centrica.com
International Power	www.ipplc.com
Johnson Matthey	www.matthey.com
Network Rail	www.networkrail.co.uk
Scottish and Southern Energy	www.scottish-southern.com
Sutton Harbour Holdings	www.sutton-harbour.co.uk
Tesco	www.tesco.com
Unilever	www.unilever.com
Vodafone Group	www.vodafone.com

ANNUAL REPORT SERVICES

CAROL   www.carol.co.uk
Financial Times   www.ar.wilink.com

CAROL, as the acronym suggests, provides direct links to company annual reports online.

COMMERCIAL DATABASES OF ACCOUNTING AND FINANCIAL DATA

Company Analysis
Datastream
Extel Financials
Thomson Financial
Worldscope

All of these databases are controlled by Thomson Financial (www.thomson.com/solutions/financial) and are available by subscription.

6

Profitability, Return on Investment and Value Added

For what is Worth in anything
But so much Money as 'twill bring.

Samuel Butler, *Hudibras*, I, i

PROFITABILITY

One of the first questions that a shareholder is likely to ask of a company is whether it is making a profit. If so, is it making a satisfactory profit? We have already encountered some of the difficulties that arise in trying to measure profit. Although accountants try to ensure that measurements are as reliable and relevant as possible, many financial numbers, even those purporting to represent past events, are necessarily to some extent estimates. Profit calculations are especially affected by the difficulties of measuring depreciation, amortization, impairment, inventories and provisions, difficulties that are accentuated in times of changing price levels and fluctuating exchange rates.

RETURN ON INVESTMENT

Profits should not be looked at in isolation from the investment made to achieve them. Investment can be defined both from a proprietary point of view and an entity point of view (see Chapter 2). This leads to a distinction between return on equity (ROE) and return on net assets

(ROA). The first ratio is a measure of the profitability of the investment made by the ordinary shareholders:

$$\text{Return on equity (ROE)} = \frac{\text{earnings}}{\text{shareholders' equity}}$$

where earnings refers to profit attributable to the ordinary shareholders (see the discussion of earnings per share in Chapter 8), and shareholders' equity excludes preference shares and minority interests.

Return on assets (ROA), on the other hand, relates operating profit to total assets less current liabilities:

$$\text{Return on assets (ROA)} = \frac{\text{operating profit}}{\text{total assets less current liabilities}}$$

Total assets less current liabilities is of course equal in amount to shareholders' equity plus non-current liabilities.

Both ratios have their uses. The difference between them is that ROA removes the effects of taxation and the way in which the company is financed. ROA is the easier to decompose:

$$\text{Return on assets (ROA)} = \frac{\text{operating profit}}{\text{sales}} \times \frac{\text{sales}}{\text{total assets less current liabilities}}$$

Return on equity and return on assets are calculated for BPI and Johnson Matthey in Table 6.1. The decomposition of ROA for those companies is shown in Table 6.2.

Table 6.1 illustrates the difference between ROE and ROA. BPI's ROE and ROA differ much more from each other than those of Johnson Matthey do. Why is this? The explanation must lie in the capital structure of the two companies. As shown in Table 8.1 on page 90, BPI has proportionately more debt than Johnson Matthey. In 2004, its ROE was 76% greater than its ROA; in 2005, a more profitable year, it was 126%. By comparison, Johnson Matthey's ROE and ROA were identical in 2005 and only 12% different in 2006. Table 6.2 shows that it was increased operating profit margins rather than improved asset turnover that boosted ROA for both companies.

Table 6.1 Calculation of ROA and ROE

	Operating profit	Earnings	Total assets less current liabilities	Shareholders' equity	ROA	ROE
	(a)	(b)	(c)	(d)	(e) = (a)/(c)	(f) = (b)/(d)
	£m	£m	£m	£m	%	%
BPI						
2004	13.7	8.1	107.1	36.0	12.8	22.5
2005	23.3	14.2	137.4	37.0	17.0	38.4
Johnson Matthey						
2005	179.9	115.5	1,438.8	922.4	12.5	12.5
2006	228.7	152.1	1,611.1	1,038.1	14.2	14.7

Table 6.2 Decomposition of ROA

	Sales	Operating profit	Total assets less current liabilities	Operating profit margin	Asset turnover	ROA
	(a)	(b)	(c)	(d) = (b)/(a)	(e) = (a)/(c)	(f) = (b)/(c)
	£m	£m	£m	%		%
BPI						
2004	359.4	13.7	107.1	3.8	3.4	12.8
2005	410.2	23.3	137.4	5.7	3.0	17.0
Johnson Matthey						
2005	4,626.2	179.9	1,438.8	3.9	3.2	12.5
2006	4,755.9	228.7	1,611.1	4.8	3.0	14.2

ANALYSING THE INCOME STATEMENT

The details given in the consolidated income statement and the notes thereto provide opportunities for further analysis. However, as discussed in Chapter 4, the IFRS standard-setters are not very interested in formats, so the details vary between companies and can be difficult to compare.

Table 6.3 sets out turnover, each category of expense, and each profit measure for the BPI Group for the years 2004 and 2005. The meaning of the figures in this raw state is rather difficult to grasp. The figures are therefore also presented as percentages of turnover. The table shows a general improvement in the group's performance between the two years.

Table 6.3 Turnover, Expenses and Profits, BPI Group, 2004 and 2005

	2005 £m	%	2004 £m	%
Turnover	410.2	100	359.4	100
Cost of sales	(338.7)	(83)	(300.5)	(84)
Gross profit	71.5	17	58.9	16
Distribution costs	(17.4)	(4)	(16.1)	(4)
Selling and administration expenses	(28.7)	(7)	(28.2)	(8)
Profit from operations before employee profit sharing scheme	25.4	6	14.6	4
Amount applied to employee profit sharing scheme	(2.1)	(1)	(0.9)	(0)
Profit from operations	23.3	6	13.7	4
Net financing costs	(3.6)	(1)	(2.7)	(1)
Profit before tax	19.7	5	11.0	3
Tax	(5.4)	(1)	(2.9)	(1)
Profit for the year	14.3	3	8.1	2
Attributable to:				
Equity holders of the parent	14.2	3	8.1	2
Minority interests	0.1	0	–	0

Most listed companies operate in several different lines of business and in many different countries. A segmental analysis of income statement figures by line of business and by geographical region is essential. The number of such segments and the presentation of segment information vary considerably from company to company. For example Tesco in 2006 reported one line of business (retail) and three geographical segments (UK, rest of Europe, Asia), whereas by contrast BG in 2005 reported five lines of business (exploration and production; liquefied natural gas; transmission and distribution; power generation; other activities) and five geographical segments (Europe; South America; Asia and Middle East; North America and the Caribbean; Mediterranean Basin and Africa). UK companies differ greatly in the extent to which they sell in and make profits (or losses) in world markets. Two of the world's most 'transnational' companies (Vodaphone and BP) are based in the UK.

Table 6.4 summarizes segmental data for Cadbury Schweppes in 2004 and 2005. The dependence of this UK-based company on sales overseas, especially the US, is very apparent, as is also the considerable variation in segmental operating margins.

Table 6.4 Segmental Analysis, Cadbury Schweppes, 2004 and 2005

a) *By line of business*

| | 2004 | | | 2005 | | |
| | Turnover | Operating profit | Operating margin | Turnover | Operating profit | Operating margin |
	£m	£m	%	£m	£m	%
American Beverages	1,686	479	28.4	1,781	537	30.1
American Confectionery	1,093	100	9.1	1,228	153	12.4
Europe, Middle East & Africa	2,246	307	13.7	2,333	334	14.3
Asia Pacific	1,050	114	10.9	1,157	143	12.3
Central	10	(175)	n/a	9	(164)	n/a
	6,085	825		6,508	1,003	

b) *Turnover by geographical region*

| | 2004 | | 2005 | |
	£m	%	£m	%
United Kingdom	1,065	18	1,083	17
Euro Zone	602	10	588	9
United States of America	1,889	31	1,998	31
Central and Southern America	549	9	658	10
Australia	675	11	741	11
Other	1,305	21	1,440	22
	6,085	100	6,508	100

CONSTRUCTING A VALUE ADDED STATEMENT

The data provided in annual reports makes it possible not only to calculate financial ratios but also to construct additional financial statements. An example is the value added statement, which is of interest to employees, trade unions and economists, rather than shareholders. Technically, a statement of value added is merely another way of displaying the figures used to compile the income statement and the SORIE, but with the emphasis on gross value added instead of profit. Gross value added is equal in amount to turnover less bought-in materials and services. It is gross because depreciation and amortization are not included in the calculation of bought-in goods and services. The change of emphasis shifts the focus by implying that maximizing profit is not the sole purpose of a company's operations. Companies seldom publish these statements in their annual reports. Table 6.5 shows how one can be constructed from information available in published income statements.

Table 6.5 Value Added Statement, BPI Group, 2004 and 2005

	2005 £m	%	2004 £m	%
Turnover	410.2	360	359.4	353
Bought-in materials and services	296.1	260	257.5	253
Gross value added	114.1	100	101.9	100
Applied as follows:				
To employees	77.9	68	74.9	73
To providers of capital				
borrowing costs	3.2		2.9	
dividends to BPI shareholders	5.4		5.4	
minority share	0.1		0.0	
		8		8
To government as taxation	5.4	5	2.9	3
To retentions for replacement and expansion				
depreciation and amortization	13.3		13.1	
profit for the year net of dividends	8.8		2.7	
		19		16
	114.1	100	101.9	100

Explanation:

1. Turnover, minority share, taxation as in Table 6.3.
2. Bought-in materials and services = cost of sales + distribution costs + selling and administration expenses (all as in Table 6.3) – employment costs – depreciation and amortization.
3. To employees: staff costs as disclosed in annual report (including employee profit sharing scheme and interest on pension liabilities net of expected return on pension scheme assets).
4. Borrowing costs: net financing costs as in Table 6.3 excluding interest on pension liabilities net of expected return on pension scheme assets.

ANALYSING A VALUE ADDED STATEMENT

Table 6.5 discloses that 68% of gross value added went to employees in 2005 compared to 73% in 2004. Providers of capital received 8% in both years. The gainers in percentage terms were the taxation authorities and the retentions for replacement and expansion.

A number of useful ratios can be calculated from a value added statement. The ratio of gross value added to turnover provides a measure of vertical integration, i.e. of the extent to which a group of companies produces its own materials and distributes its own products as distinct from buying these goods and services from other companies. The higher the ratio the greater the extent of vertical integration. BPI's ratio (28% in both years) is relatively low. Gross value added per £1 of employment costs was £1.36 in 2004 and £1.46 in 2005. Gross value added per employee was £33,703 in 2004 and £38,902 in 2005. (The number of employees is disclosed in the notes.) The more technically advanced the industry, the higher these figures are likely to be.

7

Liquidity and Cash Flows

One may not doubt that, somehow, good
Shall come of water and of mud;
And, sure, the reverent eye must see
A purpose in liquidity.

Rupert Brooke, 'Heaven'

NATURE AND IMPORTANCE OF LIQUIDITY

Companies need to be not only profitable but also liquid. In particular, companies that are profitable in the long term must make sure that they do not fail through lack of liquidity in the short term. An increase in profits must by definition lead to a corresponding increase in a company's net assets. There is no reason, however, why its liquid assets, such as cash at bank, should automatically increase. A profitable and fast-expanding company may find that it has tied up so much of its assets in property, plant and equipment, inventories and accounts receivable (debtors) that it has difficulty in paying its accounts payable (creditors) as they fall due. To help prevent such a situation a company should prepare a cash budget. A cash budget is a plan of future cash receipts and payments, based on specific assumptions about such things as sales growth, credit terms, issues of shares or debentures, and expansion of plant. A simple example, demonstrating how a profitable company can run into liquidity problems, is given below. The example also illustrates the cash conversion cycle, the process in which cash is used to obtain inventory which is then sold on credit or for cash, and the accounts receivable converted into cash, which is then used to buy inventory.

Oodnadatta Ltd is formed on 1 January to make boomerangs at a cost of £1.50 each and sell them for £2 each. All bills are paid immediately and debts are collected within thirty days. The boomerangs manufactured and paid for in January, for example, will be sold in February and the cash proceeds collected in March. The company's provisional plans are to sell 400 boomerangs in February, 600 in March, 800 in April and so on. At 1 January the company has £600 in cash (raised by an issue of shares) – just sufficient to pay for the making of the first 400 boomerangs – but no other assets.

Before starting production, the company draws up monthly budgets relating to profits and cash flows (Table 7.1). The figures show that, although the planned profit for the year is £7,700, cash will fall by £1,000 from a positive £600 to a negative £400. There is thus £8,700 to be accounted for. We can see what will happen by comparing the balance sheet at 1 January with that at 31 December (Table 7.2). The difference column in the table shows the position quite clearly. All the profits (£7,700), plus the original cash (£600) plus another £400 are tied up in accounts receivable and inventory. However, by the end of next January the company's liquidity crisis will be over:

	31 January £
Balance at beginning of month	− 400
Cash in: accounts receivable	+4,800
	+4,400
Cash out: accounts payable	−4,200
	+ 200

The catch is, of course, that as a result of its 'overtrading' the company is unlikely to reach next January, in spite of its excellent profit-making potential, unless it can raise more cash by borrowing, by collecting its debts faster or by keeping down the size of its inventory.

If sales continue to rise and costs also remain the same, the company will run into the opposite problem: excess liquidity. The purpose of drawing up cash budgets is to ensure that a company neither runs out of cash, nor keeps cash idle when it could be profitably invested.

Table 7.1 Oodnadatta Ltd: Cash Budget and Budgeted Income Statement

Budgeted income statement

	Jan. £	Feb. £	Mar. £	Apr. £	May £	June £	July £	Aug. £	Sep. £	Oct. £	Nov. £	Dec. £	Total £
Sales	—	800	1,200	1,600	2,000	2,400	2,800	3,200	3,600	4,000	4,400	4,800	30,800
Cost of sales	—	600	900	1,200	1,500	1,800	2,100	2,400	2,700	3,000	3,300	3,600	23,100
Profit	—	200	300	400	500	600	700	800	900	1,000	1,100	1,200	7,700

Note. The sales figures are equal to the quantity sold multiplied by £2; the cost of sales figures to the quantity sold multiplied by £1.50; the profit figures to the quantity sold multiplied by £0.50. The cost of sales figures give the cost of the goods *sold* during the month, *not* the cost of the goods *manufactured*.

Cash Budget

	Jan. £	Feb. £	Mar. £	Apr. £	May £	June £	July £	Aug. £	Sep. £	Oct. £	Nov. £	Dec. £
Balance at beginning of month	+ 600	—	– 900	– 1,300	– 1,600	– 1,600	– 1,800	– 1,900	– 1,900	– 1,800	– 1,600	– 1,300
Cash received from debtors	—	—	+ 800	+ 1,200	+ 1,600	+ 2,000	+ 2,400	+ 2,800	+ 3,200	+ 3,600	+ 4,000	+ 4,400
	+ 600	– 900	– 100	– 100	—	+ 200	+ 500	+ 900	+ 1,400	+ 2,000	+ 2,700	+ 3,500
Cash paid to creditors	– 600	– 900	– 1,200	– 1,500	– 1,800	– 2,100	– 2,400	– 2,700	– 3,000	– 3,300	– 3,600	– 3,900
Balance at end of month	—	– 900	– 1,300	– 1,600	– 1,800	– 1,900	– 1,900	– 1,800	– 1,600	– 1,300	– 900	– 400

Note. Cash received from debtors is equal to the sales of the previous month; cash payments to creditors to the cost of sales of the next month.

Table 7.2 Oodnadatta Ltd: Balance Sheets, 1 January and 31 December

	1 January £	31 December £	Difference £
Cash	+ 600	− 400	− 1,000
Accounts receivable	—	+ 4,800	+ 4,800
Inventory	—	+ 3,900	+ 3,900
	+ 600	+ 8,300	+ 7,700
Share capital	+ 600	+ 600	—
Retained profits	—	+ 7,700	+ 7,700
	+ 600	+ 8,300	+ 7,700

MEASURES OF LIQUIDITY

Cash budgets are unavailable to the external financial analyst, who must therefore make use of less precise measures. Such measures can be derived from the main financial statements or from the relationships between them. What the analyst tries to do is to approximate the possible future cash flows as closely as possible. A number of measures have been devised. These include current and liquid ratios and the defensive or no-credit interval, which are described and illustrated below. Since liquidity depends in part on how quickly debts are collected, bills are paid and inventory turned over, we also look at measures relating to the other components of the cash conversion cycle: accounts receivable and payable (debtors and creditors) and inventory.

CURRENT AND LIQUID RATIOS

The most traditional measure of liquidity is the current ratio, which is calculated as follows:

$$\text{current ratio} = \frac{\text{current assets}}{\text{current liabilities}}$$

The idea behind the ratio is to compare the company's cash and other assets expected to be converted into cash within a company's normal operating cycle with the company's liabilities expected to have to be paid within that cycle (often equated with one year from the date of the balance sheet).

A more immediate measure of liquidity is obtained by omitting inventories from the numerator. The resulting ratio is known as the liquid, quick or acid test ratio:

$$\text{liquid ratio} = \frac{\text{current assets} - \text{inventories}}{\text{current liabilities}}$$

The liquid ratio has the incidental advantage of being more easily compared among companies, since it does not depend, as does the current ratio, on the method chosen to value the inventories.

The calculations for BPI as at 31 December 2004 and 2005 are shown in Table 7.3.

Table 7.3 Calculation of Current and Liquid Ratios, BPI Group, 31 Dec. 2004 and 2005

	Current assets (a) £m	Inventories (b) £m	Liquid assets (c) = (a)–(b) £m	Current liabilities (d) £m	Current ratio (e) = (a)/(d)	Liquid ratio (f) = (c)/(d)
2004	121.3	58.4	62.9	104.9	1.16	0.60
2005	119.4	55.3	64.1	75.5	1.58	0.85

BPI was more liquid at the end of 2005 than at the end of 2004. The reason was the decrease in current liabilities. Looking at the detail of these liabilities shows that the only items that changed significantly were 'other loans and borrowings', which fell from £21.1m to £1.0m and bank overdrafts, which fell from £13.4m to £5.8m. If these are excluded from the calculations, the current and liquid ratios were very similar in both years.

These are typical ratios for a manufacturing company. A retailer, which sells for cash and buys on credit, should have lower ratios. For example, the ratios of Tesco can be calculated as in Table 7.4.

Table 7.4 Calculation of Current and Liquid Ratios, Tesco, 26 Feb. 2005 and 25 Feb. 2006

	Current assets (a)	Inventories (b)	Liquid assets (c) = (a)–(b)	Current liabilities (d)	Current ratio (e) = (a)/(d)	Liquid ratio (f) = (c)/(d)
	£m	£m	£m	£m		
2005	3,224	1,309	1,915	5,680	0.57	0.34
2006	3,919	1,464	2,455	7,518	0.52	0.33

It will be remembered from Chapter 2 that the final dividend is not recorded as a current liability. Nevertheless, final dividends are usually substantial in amount and payable within a few months of the balance sheet date. The final dividends of BPI as proposed at 31 December 2004 and 2005 were £3.6m in 2004 and £3.9m in 2005. If these are added to the current liabilities as stated in Table 7.3, the current ratios fall to 1.12 in 2004 and 1.50 in 2005, and the liquid ratios to 0.58 in 2004 and 0.81 in 2005. The proposed final dividends of Tesco were £365m in 2005 and £410m in 2006. If these are added to the current liabilities as stated in Table 7.4, the current ratios fall to 0.53 (2005) and 0.49 (2006) and the liquid ratios to 0.32 (2005) and 0.31 (2006).

DEFENSIVE OR NO-CREDIT INTERVAL

Both the current and the liquid ratios are static, in that they treat liquidity as something to be measured at a point in time rather than over a period. A more dynamic approach would be to divide the liquid assets not by the current liabilities but by those operating expenses from continuing operations which require the use of liquid assets, namely cost of sales, distribution costs and administrative expenses. Depreciation is not included as it is not a cash expense. What is sought is a crude measure of how long a company could survive without borrowing if no receipts were coming in from debtors or cash sales. The calculations for BPI in 2004 and 2005 are shown in Table 7.5. The result of the calculations can be called the defensive or no-credit interval. It would be preferable to use forecast rather than past cash expenses, but these, of course, are not available to external analysts. The defensive intervals calculated in Table 7.5 suggest, unlike the current and liquid ratios, that liquidity worsened slightly in 2005. A possible reason for this is that the defensive interval calculation ignores the fall in other loans and borrowings and bank overdrafts.

Table 7.5 Calculation of Defensive Intervals, BPI Group, 2004 and 2005

	Liquid assets (= col c, Table 7.3) (a) £m	Operating expenses requiring use of liquid assets (cost of sales, distribution costs, selling and administration expenses, excluding depreciation) (b) £m	Defensive interval (days) (c) = (a)/(b) × 365
2004	62.9	331.7	69
2005	64.1	371.5	63

AVERAGE PAYMENT PERIOD, AVERAGE COLLECTION PERIOD, INVENTORY TURNOVER

Liquidity depends in part on the speed at which debts are collected, creditors are paid and inventory is turned over. Companies are required by law to state their creditor payment policy in the Directors' Report. For example, BPI states in its 2005 Report that terms and conditions are agreed with suppliers before business takes place and the policy is to pay agreed invoices in accordance with the terms of payment. At the 2005 year end the amount owed to trade creditors was equivalent to 58 days [2004 – 60 days] of purchases from suppliers. BPI does not follow any code or standard on payment practice but it is its policy to pay all suppliers within 30 days of the end of the month in which goods or services are received unless other payment terms have been agreed. Some companies, Tesco for example, are signatories to the Confederation of British Industry (CBI) Code of Prompt Payment.

Disclosure is very helpful because average payment periods are difficult to calculate in the absence of a figure for purchases in company reports. The formula is:

$$\text{average payment period} = \frac{\text{average trade creditors} \times 365 \text{ days}}{\text{credit purchases}}$$

Companies disclose not purchases but cost of sales. Since, however, the cost of goods sold is equal to cost of goods purchased plus opening inventories minus closing inventories, a purchases figure can be estimated if it is assumed that all purchases are made on credit, not for cash. Figures for opening and closing trade creditors are always disclosed in the Notes. The calculation for BPI in 2005 is shown in Table 7.6. The result is very close but not identical to that made by the company itself.

Table 7.6 Calculation of Average Payment Period, BPI Group 2005

Cost of sales	Change in raw materials inventory	Purchases	Average trade creditors	Average payment period
(a)	(b)	(c)	(d)	(e)=(d)/(c) × 365
£m	£m	£m	£m	days
338.7	(4.1)	334.6	52.15	57

The requirement to disclose average payment periods derives from allegations that some large companies are very slow in paying their suppliers. Company law does not require the disclosure of average collection periods. The formula is:

$$\text{average collection period} = \frac{\text{average trade debtors} \times 365 \text{ days}}{\text{credit sales}}$$

One problem with this ratio is that debtors include value added tax (VAT), whereas sales do not. The calculation for BPI in 2005 is given in Table 7.7. It is assumed that all the group's sales are credit sales, not cash sales – a reasonable assumption for BPI, but not, of course, for a retailer such as Tesco.

Table 7.7 Calculation of Average Collection Period, BPI Group 2005

Sales	Average trade debtors	Average collection period
(a)	(b)	(c) = (b)/(a) × 365
£m	£m	days
410.2	60.45	54

Another way of looking at the average collection period would be to think in terms of debtors turnover:

$$\text{debtors turnover} = \frac{\text{sales}}{\text{average debtors}}$$

The relationship between inventories and cost of sales is usually thought of in this way:

$$\text{inventory turnover} = \frac{\text{cost of sales}}{\text{average inventory}}$$

The inventory turnover of BPI is calculated in Table 7.8.

Table 7.8 Calculation of Inventory Turnover, BPI Group 2005

Cost of sales	Average inventory	Inventory turnover	Inventory turnover in days
(a)	(b)	(c) = (a)/(b)	(d) = 365/(c)
£m	£m	£m	days
338.7	56.85	5.96	61

The cash conversion cycle equals inventory turnover plus debt collection period minus average payment period expressed in days. For BPI in 2005, this was 61 + 54 − 57 = 58.

In assessing these ratios it must be remembered that they are weighted averages. There may be important differences per line of business and per geographical region which only more detailed accounts would reveal.

PREDICTING INSOLVENCY

The extreme case of illiquidity is insolvency, which occurs when a company is unable to pay its debts as they fall due.

Can financial ratios be used to predict insolvency? Researchers have approached this problem by examining the ratios of failed companies just prior to insolvency. It is possible by the use of statistical techniques to calculate what is known as a 'Z score' based on a number of relevant ratios appropriately weighted. Companies with scores within a certain range are more likely to become insolvent.

As is usual in ratio analysis, it is necessary to use more than one ratio, and the result is a guide, not a certainty. A company with a bad score is not certain to become insolvent, only more likely to.

WINDOW-DRESSING

We end this chapter with a problem that arises from the nature of ratios. If companies are judged by the ratios that can be calculated from their financial statements, there may be a temptation to present statements which, within the limits possible, produce favourable rather than unfavourable ratios. In the context of current and liquid ratios, this form of creative accounting is known as window-dressing, the manipulation of ratios to give a misleading impression. It can be illustrated by a simplified example.

Suppose that a company has current assets of £800m, current liabilities of £500m and liquid assets of £550m. Its *net* current assets and *net* liquid assets will therefore be £300m and £50m respectively. If we keep these net amounts constant but vary the gross amounts by using liquid assets to pay off current liabilities, the current and liquid ratios will vary as shown in Table 7.9. The example is exaggerated to make a point, but it is important to note it may be possible to so arrange current assets and liabilities as to have the desired ratios at the balance sheet date.

Table 7.9 Illustration of Window-dressing

Current assets (a) £000	Current liabilities (b) £000	Liquid assets (c) £000	Current ratio (a)/(b)	Liquid ratio (c)/(b)
800	500	550	1.60	1.10
700	400	450	1.75	1.12
600	300	350	2.00	1.17
500	200	250	2.50	1.25
400	100	150	4.00	1.50
350	50	100	7.00	2.00
301	1	51	301.00	51.00

8 Sources of Funds and Capital Structure

Les affaires, c'est bien simple: c'est l'argent des autres.

Alexandre Dumas, fils, *La Question d'argent*

SOURCES OF FUNDS

The funds available to a company are obtained either from its shareholders or by borrowing. The former includes not only issues of shares but also the retention of profits. The latter ranges from long-term debt to trade credit. The composition at any time of these sources, and more especially the long-term sources, is referred to as the 'capital structure' of a company. For many companies the most important source of funds is the ordinary shareholders, especially through the medium of reserves (which include retained profits), but also through the issue of new shares. Borrowings are important, but preference shares and minority interests are of minor importance. Capital structures do however differ from company to company. Table 8.1 summarizes and compares the equity and non-current borrowing of three companies in 2005 and 2006. Johnson Matthey is less reliant on borrowings than are Scottish and Southern Energy and BPI.

Table 8.1 Comparison of Capital Structures

	BPI (31.12.05)		Johnson Matthey (31.3.06)		Scottish and Southern Energy (31.3.06)	
	£m	%	£m	%	£m	%
Share capital	6	8	220	15	430	11
Share premium and other reserves	32	41	110	7	125	3
Retained earnings	(1)	(1)	708	47	1,590	40
Shareholders' equity	37	48	1,038	69	2,145	54
Minority interests	0	0	6	1	0	0
Borrowings (non-current)	41	52	455	30	1,798	46
	78	100	1,499	100	3,943	100

CAPITAL STRUCTURE

Table 8.1 suggests that there is no one capital structure that is best for every company, but is there an optimal capital structure for a particular company? This is a question which has aroused much debate. In principle there probably is such a structure but it is not simple in practice for a company to discover what it is or to achieve it.

The main problem is to achieve the best mix of debt (loans, debentures) and equity (ordinary shares, retained profits, other reserves). There is no easy way of doing this. It is possible to list the factors which ought to be considered, but assessing the weight to be given to each remains very much a matter of judgement and experience. The factors are:

1. *Cost* The current and future cost of each potential source of capital should be estimated and compared. The costs of each source are not necessarily independent of each other. An increase in debt now, for example, may push up the cost of equity later. Other things being equal, it is desirable to minimize the average cost of capital to the company.
2. *Risk* It is unwise (and often disastrous) to place a company in a position where it may be unable, even if profits fall only temporarily, to pay interest as it falls due or to pay back loans. It is also undesirable

to be forced to cut or omit the ordinary dividend (see the section below on dividend policy).

3. *Control* Except where there is no alternative, a company should not make any issue of shares which will have the effect of removing or diluting the control of the existing shareholders.

4. *Acceptability* A company can only borrow if others are willing to lend to it. Few listed companies can afford the luxury of a capital structure that is unacceptable to financial institutions. A company with readily mortgageable assets and/or reliable cash flows will find it easier to raise debt.

5. *Transferability* Shares may be listed or unlisted. Many companies have made issues to the public in order to obtain a stock exchange listing and improve the transferability of their shares. Such a procedure may also have tax advantages. On the other hand, listed companies are increasingly subject to regulations that dictate a transparency that may not be to the liking of some directors and shareholders, who may therefore prefer to avoid listed status.

Cost of capital and risk are discussed in more detail in the next two sections.

COST OF CAPITAL

Although a company cannot always choose what appears to be the cheapest source of capital, because of the need to pay attention to risk, control, acceptability and transferability, it should always estimate the cost of each potential source and the effect on the overall average cost.

An oversimplified approach is to work out first of all the cost of each potential source of capital. This is most easily done for loans and debentures. Suppose that a company can issue £100,000 10 per cent debentures at par, repayable at par in twenty years' time. The before tax cost is obviously 10 per cent; the after tax cost, assuming a corporation tax rate of 30 per cent, is 7 per cent. If preference shares are issued instead, the before and after tax rates would be equal, since preference dividends, unlike debenture interest, are not deductible for tax purposes. This explains why, following the introduction of corporation tax in 1965, many companies replaced their preference shares by loan stock.

The arithmetic becomes rather more difficult if the loan stock is not issued at par. Suppose, for example, an issue made in 2001, of £40 million 10.75 per cent unsecured loan stock 2026 at £98 per cent. That is, for every £98 received in 2001, a company promises to pay interest of £10.75 each year and to redeem (repay) the stock at par (£100) in 2026. It can be calculated that the yield to redemption is about 11 per cent. The real cost of issuing debentures would be reduced during a period of inflation since the cash paid out by the company would have a lower purchasing power than the cash it receives at the date of issue.

Reckoning the cost of an issue of ordinary shares is more difficult. An analogous calculation to the one above would suggest that the cost is equal to the dividend yield, worked out as follows:

$$\frac{\text{current dividend per ordinary share} \times 100}{\text{market price per share}}$$

Dividend yields may be found in the stock exchange pages of the *Financial Times* and other newspapers, and on the internet. The *Financial Times* London Share Service gives a lot of information about shares every day. The following typical entry relating to the chemicals company Johnson Matthey has been extracted from the *Financial Times* of 6 September 2006 (referring to the day before):

	Price	Chng	52 week High	Low	Yld	P/E
Johnson Matthey	£13.66	+0.08	£15.35	£10.99	2.2	18.6

This tells us (for the date in question) that the current market price of Johnson Matthey's ordinary shares (par value £1) is £13.66 compared with a high over the last 52 weeks of £15.35, a low of £10.99 and a price for the day before of £13.58.

Johnson Matthey's dividend yield is calculated as follows:

$$\frac{30.1 \times 100}{1366} = 2.20\%$$

where 30.1p is the dividend per share as stated in the company's 2006 annual report.

The dividend yield of any company can be compared to dividend yields in general and with those of other companies in the same equity sector or sub-sector by looking in the table in the *Financial Times* headed

FTSE Actuaries Share Indices. On 5 September 2006 the dividend yield for Chemicals was 2.24%. These yields can be compared with the yields on other listed companies and the average yield (3.24%) on the companies composing the FTSE ('Footsie') 100 share index (of which Johnson Matthey is a constituent member).

The dividend yield cannot, however, be regarded as an adequate measure of the cost of equity capital. It fails to take account of the facts that future dividends may be different from the current dividend and that the price of the shares may change. Neither of these considerations is relevant to long-term debt with its fixed interest payments and fixed redemption prices.

Two possible measures of the cost of equity capital are the earnings yield and the dividend yield plus a growth rate. The earnings yield is calculated as follows:

$$\frac{\text{earnings per share after tax} \times 100}{\text{market price per ordinary share}}$$

It is more usual to express the same relationship in the form of a price–earnings ratio (P/E ratio), which is simply the reciprocal of the earnings yield multiplied by 100, that is:

$$\frac{\text{market price per ordinary share}}{\text{earnings per ordinary share after tax}}$$

In other words, the P/E ratio expresses the multiple of the last reported earnings that the market is willing to pay for the ordinary shares. The higher the P/E ratio (the lower the earnings yield) the more the market thinks of the company and the cheaper the cost of equity capital to the company. From the extract from the *Financial Times* it can be seen that the P/E ratio of Johnson Matthey on 5 September 2006 was 18.6. How this figure was calculated is explained in the next section.

EARNINGS PER SHARE

The calculation of basic earnings per share (EPS) (already briefly referred to in Chapter 2) can be illustrated from the 2006 annual report of Johnson Matthey:

$$\text{basic EPS} = \frac{\text{profit attributable to equity shareholders of the parent company}}{\text{weighted number of ordinary shares in issue during the year}}$$

$$= \frac{152,100,000 \times 100}{214,895,523} = 70.8 \text{ pence}$$

The P/E ratio on 5 September 2006 using basic EPS was therefore:

$$\frac{\text{market price per share}}{\text{basic EPS}} = \frac{1366.0}{70.8} = 19.3$$

For several reasons, the P/E ratio thus calculated is often slightly different from the ratio reported in the *Financial Times*. Basic EPS is a simple calculation which most annual reports immediately amplify and qualify. First, total basic EPS is split between continuing operations and discontinued operations. (Johnson Matthey's total and continuing operations basic EPS were identical in 2006 but not in 2005.) Secondly, companies are required to publish, where appropriate, a 'diluted' as well as a 'basic' EPS. Dilution can arise from the existence of shares that may rank for dividends in the future such as loans convertible into ordinary shares and options and warrants (see below). Johnson Matthey published a diluted EPS of 70.5p which recognizes that EPS would look worse after taking account of the share options granted to senior employees and a long-term incentive plan encouraging those employees to buy shares in the company. Thirdly, and most important in the present context, many companies and investment analysts argue that earnings should be calculated before 'exceptional items', i.e. those within the ordinary activities of the business but of unusual size or incidence. In 2006 Johnson Matthey included impairment losses and restructuring costs, net of tax, in this category and reported a 'headline' EPS before exceptional items of 72.7p (basic) and 72.4p (diluted). Fourthly, the *Financial Times* may make use of information not available at the time of publication of the annual report. Both headline EPS and basic EPS are featured in the financial highlights section on the second page of Johnson Matthey's 2006 annual report and all calculations are fully spelled out in the notes to the income statement.

Because of the way the UK tax system works, there is a distinction between the 'net basis' and the 'nil basis' of calculating EPS. The tax charge depends to some extent on the amount of dividends declared, giving rise to both constant and variable components. The net basis takes account of both components and has the advantage that all relevant facts are considered. The nil basis takes account only of the constant components. assuming in effect a nil distribution of dividends. Its advantage is that it produces an EPS that is independent of the level of dividend distribution. For most companies the two bases will in practice give the same result, but this is not likely for companies relying heavily on overseas income. The *Financial Times* calculates P/E ratios on a net basis.

The relationship between EPS and dividend per share (DPS) is known as dividend cover. Johnson Matthey's total dividend for 2005 was 30.1p per share, so its dividend cover (using headline EPS) was

$$\frac{\text{EPS}}{\text{DPS}} = \frac{72.7}{30.1} = 2.4$$

The DPS is the sum of the interim dividend paid in 2005 and the final dividend proposed and payable in 2006, even though the latter is not shown as a current liability in the balance sheet. DPS is thus not equal to the total dividends paid during the financial year.

Since the market is interested in future dividends, it prefers to see current dividends reasonably well covered by current earnings. This is some sort of guarantee that the dividends will be maintained in future, since if profits fall there will be retained profits to draw upon. There is a discussion of divided policy later in this chapter.

An alternative approach to the cost of equity capital is to add a growth rate to the dividend yield. If one considers, for example, that Johnson Matthey's dividends are likely to grow in future at an average annual rate of 5 per cent, then its cost of equity capital would be estimated to be 2.2 per cent plus 5 per cent or 7.2 per cent.

A more sophisticated approach to calculating the cost of equity capital is to use the capital asset pricing model (CAPM). Using a set of restrictive assumptions, the cost of a company's equity capital is equal to

$$R_f + \beta \left[E\left(R_m\right) - R_f \right]$$

where R_f is the return on a riskless security (e.g. a treasury bill), $E\left(R_m\right)$ is the expected return on all the securities in the market (known as the market portfolio) and β (beta) is a measure of risk.

The meaning and measurement of beta are discussed in the next section.

RISK: BETAS AND GEARING

Risk is of two kinds: market (or systematic) risk and specific (or non-market) risk. Market risk can be quantified as the beta of a company's ordinary shares. Beta measures the sensitivity of the share price to movements in the market. Johnson Matthey's beta was estimated by the London Business School Risk Measurement Service (RMS) (Oct.–Dec. 2006 issue) to be 1.03. A beta of 1.03 means that the share will on average move 1.03 per cent for each 1 per cent move by the market. A share with a beta of 1.0 would on average move in line with the market. Betas as reported by RMS ranged from 0.07 to 1.84. The beta of the Royal Bank of Scotland (RBS), for example, was 1.26. Industry betas are also available: 0.95 for speciality chemicals and 1.06 for banks, if the component companies are equally weighted.

Specific risk refers to factors specific to a company and is measured as a percentage return per annum. The higher the percentage, the greater the specific risk. Investment trusts (companies which invest in the securities of other companies) tend to have the lowest specific risk. Specific risk figures ranged from 3 per cent to 185 per cent. Johnson Matthey's and RBS's figures were 14 per cent and 16 per cent respectively. The industry figures were 47 per cent and 19 per cent on an equally weighted basis.

The distinction between market risk and specific risk is important, because it is possible to reduce the latter by diversification (e.g. by holding shares in both speciality chemical manufacturers and banks) but market risk cannot be diversified away. Both Johnson Matthey and RBS are affected by the state of the economy in which they operate.

Betas can be measured from either market data ('market betas') or accounting data ('accounting betas'). Betas do, of course, change over time but most are reasonably stationary.

The more traditional accounting measure of risk is gearing. Companies with the highest betas tend to be highly geared and to come from highly cyclical industries. Gearing (or 'leverage' as the Americans call it) is the relationship between the funds provided to a company by its shareholders and those provided by lenders. The latter are often defined as long-term sources of funds carrying a fixed interest charge or dividend (e.g. unsecured loans, debentures and preference shares). The degree of gearing can be measured in terms of either capital or income. A company's capital structure is said to be highly geared when the fixed charges claim an above average proportion of the company's resources of either capital or income.

There are several ways of defining and calculating a 'gearing ratio' and it is important when making comparisons to know which definitions are being used. Whichever way the calculations are made, some companies are more highly geared than others. Companies that have relatively stable cash flows and/or assets that can be specifically identified and are not likely to suffer impairment losses over time (thereby providing good security) find it easier to borrow. One definition of the ratio is:

$$\frac{\text{non-current interest-bearing liabilities} + \text{preference shares} \times 100\%}{\text{ordinary shareholders' equity} + \text{minority interests}}$$

Using this definition, the gearing ratios of the companies in Table 8.1 are:

	%
BPI	111
Johnson Matthey	44
Scottish and Southern Energy	84

All three companies have no preference shares and insignificant minority interests.

Some companies, e.g. International Power, calculate a gearing ratio using 'net debt' as the numerator and net assets (equal in amount to parent shareholders' equity plus minority interest) as the denominator. Net debt is usually defined as loans (both current and non-current) after the deduction of cash and cash equivalents. The rationale for *net* debt is that the cash and cash equivalents are available to pay off the loans. If cash and cash equivalents exceed loans, this ratio will be negative. To calculate the gearing ratios of the companies in Table 8.1 using this definition we need additional data, as follows:

	BPI (31.12.05) £m	Johnson Matthey (31.3.06) £m	Scottish and Southern Energy (31.3.06) £m
Borrowings (current)	7	90	417
Cash and cash equivalents	1	133	50

The gearing ratios re-calculated are:

	%
BPI	127
Johnson Matthey	40
Scottish and Southern Energy	101

The ranking of the companies is unchanged but BPI and SSE appear to be more highly geared than under the previous definition.

'Times interest earned' (also known as interest cover) looks at gearing from the point of view of the income statement rather than the balance sheet. It is usually defined as:

$$\frac{\text{profit before interest and tax}}{\text{interest (before tax)}}$$

The lower this ratio, the more highly geared the company is. Definitions of the numerator and the denominator vary. The purpose of the calculation is to gauge the extent to which this year's profit from operations covers this year's interest payable. Since interest payable can be paid off by interest receivable it seems preferable to define the denominator as net financing costs (although still of course before tax). Interest on pension liabilities and expected returns on pension scheme assets are ignored since they are unconnected with operations. Shares of profits of associates and joint ventures are excluded because they are unlikely to be available in cash.

Using the above definitions, the calculations for the companies in Table 8.1 are shown in Table 8.2.

Table 8.2 Calculation of Times Interest Earned

	BPI	Johnson Matthey	Scottish & Southern Energy
Profit before interest and tax	£23.3m	£228.7m	£942.7
Net interest payable (before tax)	£3.2m	£14.7m	£105.1
Times interest earned	7.3	15.6	9.0

In contrast to the balance sheet-based gearing ratios, BPI appears less highly geared. This is because of its good profit figures in 2005. In 2004, when its profit before tax and interest was £13.7m and interest payable

£2.9m, its times interest earned figure was 4.7. A disadvantage of the method is that it ignores the existence of retained profits built up in previous years, upon which the company could call if necessary (if they are in liquid form). The same drawback applies to the 'priority percentages' approach, in which the analyst calculates the percentage of earnings that is required to service each category of loan and share capital.

The effect of gearing on the profits available to ordinary shareholders can be seen from the following example.

X PLC is a very highly geared company and Y PLC a relatively low-geared one. Their long-term sources of funds at the beginning of the year are as follows:

	X	Y
	£	£
Ordinary share capital (par value)	100,000	200,000
Retained profits	100,000	200,000
Ordinary shareholders' equity	200,000	400,000
10% debenture	300,000	100,000
	500,000	500,000
Gearing ratio (debenture as a percentage of ordinary shareholders' equity)	150%	25%

If the earnings (profit) before interest and tax (EBIT) during the year is £80,000 for both companies, the distributable profit will be as follows, assuming a 30 per cent tax rate:

	X	Y
	£	£
(a) Profit before interest and tax	80,000	80,000
(b) Debenture interest (gross)	30,000	10,000
	50,000	70,000
Tax at 30%	15,000	21,000
	35,000	49,000
Times interest earned (a/b)	2.67	8.00

Distributable profit will be 35% of the par value for company X and 24.5% for Company Y.

If, however, the profit before interest and tax is £160,000, the position will be as follows:

	X	Y
	£	£
(a) Profit before interest and tax	160,000	160,000
(b) Debenture interest (gross)	30,000	10,000
	130,000	150,000
Tax at 30%	39,000	91,000
	91,000	105,000
Times interest earned (a/b)	5.33	16.00

Distributable profit as a proportion of the par value becomes 91% for Company X and 52.5% for Company Y. Note that while profit before interest and tax has doubled, X's distributable profit as a percentage of par value has gone up 2.6 times and Y's 2.14 times (because Y is less highly geared than X). It is clear that gearing enables a company to trade on the equity, as the Americans say, and to increase the ordinary shareholders' return at a faster rate than the increase in profits. The higher the gearing, the greater the relative rate.

Unfortunately, the converse also applies. Suppose that the profit before interest and tax falls to £30,000. The position will then be as follows:

	X	Y
	£	£
(a) Profit before interest and tax	30,000	30,000
(b) Debenture interest (gross)	30,000	10,000
	–	20,000
Tax at 30%		6,000
		14,000
Times interest earned (a/b)	1.0	3.0

The distributable profit as a proportion of par value of Company X falls to zero and that of Company Y to 7%. If profits fell even further, Company X would not be able to pay the debenture interest out of its current profits. Company Y is in a much better position to meet such an emergency. It must also be remembered, of course (from Chapter 7), that a company that has tied up its assets too much in property, plant, equipment and inventories may run into similar difficulties even though its profits have not fallen. Profits are not the same thing as ready cash.

The moral is that companies whose profits are low, or likely to fluctuate violently, should not be highly geared. Investors in such companies are running risks and will in any case prefer ordinary shares to fixed-interest debentures. From a company point of view, the attraction of a relatively cheap source of funds must be balanced against the risks involved.

DIVIDEND POLICY

How does a company determine the size of the dividend it pays each year, or, putting the question round the other way, how does a company decide how much of its profits to retain each year?

Retained profits are the most convenient source of funds, and a company which pays very high dividends loses this source and may have to raise money in the capital market. Issues of debentures and loans have a lower cost of capital than either new issues of shares or retained profits, but, as we have just seen, there are dangers in a highly geared capital structure. New issues of share are more expensive than retained profits because of the issue costs involved. (Incidentally, retained profits are not a costless source. They are in effect a notional distribution of profits which are immediately reinvested in the company.)

On the other hand, most companies will have to go to the market sooner or later, and one of the points that potential investors will look at is the dividend record. A company whose dividend has declined or fluctuated violently is not likely to be favourably regarded. For this reason, companies prefer to maintain their dividends even if earnings fall. Dividends have an information content; that is, they confirm or alter investors' beliefs about the future prospects of a company.

On the whole, then, cost of capital considerations push companies towards constant or steadily increasing dividend payouts. Inflation may have the same effect if the directors of a company feel that the distribution to shareholders ought to keep pace with the decline in the purchasing power of money. It may also have the opposite effect if the directors feel the need to retain a higher proportion of reported earnings in order to maintain operating capacity. Two other factors that have affected the size of dividends are government policy and taxation. A number of UK governments after the Second World War, although not in recent decades, in their efforts to contain prices and wages placed statutory limitations on the size of company dividends. In spite of capital gains tax, the British tax system favours increases in capital rather than increases in income. There are many shareholders who are more interested in capital gains than in dividends. In general, shareholders are likely to be attracted to companies which have a dividend policy suited to their needs. This is known as the 'clientele effect'.

We are now in a position to look at the dividend policies of Johnson Matthey and BPI, using the EPS and DPS figures stated in their annual reports. Table 8.3 shows that Johnson Matthey's EPS has risen steadily over the period 2002 to 2006 and that the company has increased its DPS every year, maintaining a constant dividend cover of 2.4 times earnings. BPI's EPS has been more volatile, but the company has maintained DPS at the expense of dividend cover. In 2005 when profits greatly improved DPS was raised but, having regard to the size of retained profits, by a much smaller percentage than the increase in EPS.

Table 8.3 Earnings and Dividends Records

Johnson Matthey	2002	2003	2004	2005	2006
EPS	60.4p	61.8p	64.0p	67.0p	72.7p
DPS	24.6p	25.5p	26.4p	27.7p	30.1p
Dividend cover	2.5	2.4	2.4	2.4	2.4

Note: 2002–04 on a UK GAAP basis, before exceptional items and goodwill amortization; 2005–06 on an IFRS basis, before impairment losses and restructuring costs.

BPI	2001	2002	2003	2004	2005
EPS	44.05p	27.53p	29.36p	31.50p	54.28p
DPS	21.00p	21.00p	21.00p	21.00p	22.00p
Dividend cover	2.1	1.3	1.4	1.5	2.5

Note: 2001–03 on a UK GAAP basis; 2004–05 on an IFRS basis. EPS on a diluted basis.

RIGHTS ISSUES AND CAPITALIZATION ISSUES

Most major share issues are either rights issues or capitalization issues. A rights issue is one in which existing shareholders are given a chance to subscribe before anyone else. If they do not wish to do so they can sell their rights on the market. Rights issues have long been the norm, and since 1980 it has been obligatory for share issues by public companies to be rights issues unless the shareholders pass a resolution to the contrary.

In 2004 International Power issued 366 million ordinary shares at 82p per share in a 33 for 100 rights issue. Of the £286 million raised (net of expenses of £14 million), £183 million was credited to share capital and £103 million to share premium account.

A capitalization issue (also known as a 'scrip issue' or a 'bonus issue') is simply a means of turning reserves into share capital. For example, Sutton Harbour Holdings made a one for one capitalization issue in 2004, doubling its ordinary share capital but not changing the total of its shareholders' equity. To understand how this is possible consider the following simple example. X PLC's summarized balance sheet is as follows:

	£000		£000
Assets	150,000	Ordinary share capital	
		(40m shares of £1 each)	40,000
less			
Liabilities	50,000	Reserves	60,000
	£100,000		£100,000

The company decides to make a capitalization issue of one new share for two old shares. The balance sheet will now look like this:

	£000		£000
Assets	150,000	Ordinary share capital	
		(60m shares of £1 each)	60,000
less			
Liabilities	50,000	Reserves	40,000
	£100,000		£100,000

All that happened was a book entry. In order to increase the ordinary share capital from £40m to £60m, the accountant (as authorized by a resolution of the shareholders) has decreased the reserves from £60m to £40m. The shareholders have not received any cash, only more paper. Are they any better off? In principle, no: the market price *per share* might be expected to fall proportionately. In practice, it may not do so, partly because unrelated factors may be affecting share prices, partly because the rights issue may have drawn attention to the company. Of course, if the company announces at the same time that the total amount to be paid out in dividends to shareholders will be increased, then the shareholders really will receive more cash in the future.

Capitalization issues have to be adjusted for when making comparisons of earnings per share (EPS). In this example, if the earnings were £12m, the EPS before the capitalization issue would be 30p; after the issue the EPS would be 20p.

CONVERTIBLE LOAN STOCK, OPTIONS AND WARRANTS

As pointed out in Chapter 2, the distinction between debt and equity is sometimes blurred. Preference share capital, for example, obviously has some of the characteristics of long-term debt. Another security in which the distinction is blurred is the convertible loan. The attraction of such stock to investors is that it enables them to buy a fixed-interest stock which they can later change into ordinary shares if they so wish. Whether they will make the conversion or not, depends, of course, on the relationship between the market price of the ordinary shares and the price at the conversion date. The investors' hope is that they have found a cheaper way of buying the ordinary shares than direct purchase. The disadvantage is that the rate of interest offered on a convertible loan is lower than that on a 'straight' loan.

Why should a company issue convertible stock? There are at least two possibilities:

1. The company wishes to issue debt and adds the convertibility as an additional attraction.
2. The company would prefer to issue equity but believes that the price of its ordinary shares is temporarily depressed. By setting the conversion price higher than the current price, the management can, if its expectations are fulfilled, effectively make a share issue at the desired price.

The possible disadvantages to the company are that either the market price fails to rise and it is saddled with unwanted debt, or that the market price rises so quickly that it finds itself in effect selling equity more cheaply than it need have done. As already noted, the existence of convertible loan stock dilutes the basic earnings per share.

An option is a contract giving a right to buy or sell securities within or at the end of a given time period at an agreed price. Convertible loan stock is thus one form of option, as are also warrants. These are certificates giving the holder the right to purchase a security at a predetermined price at a future date or dates. The use of share options as a form of remuneration for directors and employees, and the accounting treatment thereof has already been discussed in Chapter 2.

LEASING

Instead of borrowing money to buy property, plant and equipment, a company may decide to lease them; that is, to enter into a contract which allows it the use of the assets (but does not give it the ownership) in return for a periodic rental. Early termination of the lease is penalized. Sometimes the company already owns the assets and raises cash by selling them and then leasing them back. This is known as sale-and-leaseback.

If the lease is for a long period, the economic effect in either case is similar to an issue of long-term debt, and it should be regarded and analysed as such. It has long been standard accounting practice for finance leases (those that transfer substantially all the risks and rewards of ownership to the lessee) to be capitalized. This means that both the leased asset and the liability to pay the lease rentals are shown in the balance sheet. Leases that do not transfer substantially all the risks and rewards of ownership are known as operating leases and are not capitalized. Hiring and leasing charges have to be disclosed in the notes. For example, BPI in 2005 disclosed 'interest under obligations under finance lease' of £0.2m as part of its net financing costs and 'operating lease charges' of £2.9m as part of its cost of sales.

Leases are sometimes drafted in such a way as to avoid lease capitalization since it increases reported debt. Because of this many standard-setters would prefer to treat all leases as finance leases.

OFF BALANCE SHEET FINANCING

Off balance sheet financing is the financing of a company's operations in such a way that under legal requirements and accounting standards some or all of the finance is not disclosed in its balance sheet. One effect of this is to make a company look less highly geared than it really is. Off balance sheet financing obviously has the potential to mislead users of financial statements. It has been achieved in many ingenious ways, although UK and international standard-setters have done their best to limit it. They have done so partly by banning some specific accounting treatments but also by emphasizing principles (such as having regard to the economic substance of transactions rather than their legal form) rather than rules. The more detailed a rule the more easily it can be avoided, especially when the rule involves an arbitrary percentage. This kind of avoidance has been called creative compliance.

Three examples will illustrate (in a slightly simplified fashion) the techniques and how standard-setters have sought to combat them. The first is essentially that used by the American company Enron. Debt is issued not by the parent company but by a entity set up in such a way that it does not comply with the detailed rules as to what constitutes a subsidiary although in fact the parent controls it or has the power to control it. The debt does not have to be disclosed in the *consolidated* balance sheet. This form of non-disclosure is not possible under international and UK accounting standards, since such a company is deemed to be a 'controlled special purpose entity' (IFRS terminology) or a 'quasi-subsidiary' (UK terminology), and has to be accounted for in the same way as a legal subsidiary. A second example is the issue by a subsidiary of redeemable preference shares with a dividend equal to current interest rates. At first sight, the preference shares are part of minority interest not debt in the consolidated balance sheet. However, accounting standards require that where payment of the dividends has been guaranteed by another member of the group, the shares should be recorded as debt in the consolidated balance sheet. A third example is the sale of goods by a company to a bank with a commitment or an option by the company to repurchase them at a higher amount. The form of this transaction relates solely to sales and purchases and to the income statement, but the substance of the transaction is a bank loan, especially if, as may be the case, the goods do not change their physical location. Accounting standards therefore require that the transaction be treated as a loan.

Summary and Reading Guide

The reader who has come this far has already learned a great deal about the annual reports of companies, about financial statements and about accounting and finance. The purpose of this chapter is to summarize what has been learned and to make suggestions for further reading. Most of the books mentioned are frequently revised and updated. The most recent editions should always be consulted. The Library of the Institute of Chartered Accountants in England and Wales publishes many useful reading guides. Its catalogue is available online at www.icaew.com/library.

COMPANIES AND THEIR REPORTS

Chapter 1 was mainly about companies, the most important form of business organization in modern Britain; 99.5 per cent of all companies are private but public companies (or groups of companies headed by them) are of greater economic significance. It is with public companies, and especially those listed on the London Stock Exchange, that UK investors are mainly concerned. Published annual reports are typically those of groups of companies, consisting of a parent company, subsidiaries and sub-subsidiaries.

Annual reports provide information to shareholders (the primary stakeholders) but are also used by others with a direct financial interest (e.g. lenders, trade creditors, employees: the secondary stakeholders) and by any other persons who consider themselves affected by the activities of the company (the tertiary stakeholders). Many companies with very large numbers of shareholders publish summary financial statements as well. In law, the shareholders are the owners of a company; in practice, a company is controlled by its directors. This raises problems of corporate governance, a report on which is included in the annual reports of all listed companies. Directors' remuneration is typically high and paid in many complex ways. It also is the subject of a lengthy report. Two other reports which have usually been included are an operating and financial review and a corporate social responsibility report.

The content of UK annual reports in recent years has been much influenced by membership of the European Union and by globalization. UK listed companies (and those of other EU member states) are required to comply in their consolidated financial statements with the international financial reporting standards (IFRS) promulgated by the International Accounting Standards Board (IASB).

The annual reports and financial statements of companies are prepared within a framework of company law and securities law. Two of the most stimulating and useful of the many legal textbooks and guides available are J. Dine, *Company Law* (London: Sweet & Maxwell) and R. Smerdon, *A Practical Guide to Corporate Governance* (London: Sweet & Maxwell).

FINANCIAL STATEMENTS

Chapter 2 dealt with financial statements. The four most important statements are:

1. The *balance sheet*, which shows the assets, the liabilities and the shareholders' equity at a particular date.
2. The *income statement* (or profit and loss account), which shows for an accounting period the revenues, expenses and profit (before and after taxation).
3. The *statement of recognized income and expense / statement of changes in equity*.
4. The *cash flow statement*, which shows the cash inflows and outflows for an accounting period.

The relationship between assets (A), liabilities (L) and shareholders' equity (SE) can be looked at from a proprietary (A − L = SE) or an entity (A = L + SE) point of view. Both assets and liabilities are classified into current and non-current. The net current assets (NCA) form the working capital of a company. Most UK balance sheets are set out in the vertical format: (non-current assets + NCA) − non-current liabilities = SE.

Property, plant and equipment is a tangible non-current asset. It is usually carried at historical cost (although the land and buildings element is sometimes revalued) and depreciated over its economic life by the straight line method. Depreciation, a systematic allocation over time, is distinguished from impairment, which is a recognition of a decrease in fair value.

Intangible assets have grown in importance in recent years. They include goodwill, which is not separately identifiable, and copyrights and brands, which are. Goodwill is only recognized as an asset if it is purchased; it is not amortized but is tested annually for impairment. Separately identifiable intangibles which have finite lives, such as copyrights, are amortized; separately identifiable intangibles with indefinite lives are not amortized.

Investments in associates and jointly controlled entities are usually recorded in consolidated statements using the equity method. Financial assets are classified into four categories: held for trading; held to maturity; loans and receivables; available for sale. The first category is marked to market, with fluctuations in value taken to the income statement; the second and third categories are carried in the balance sheet at amortized cost. Fluctuations in the value of the fourth are shown in the statement of recognized income and expense (SORIE) and therefore do not affect reported income. Derivatives are financial assets that derive their value from an underlying item such as a share price or an interest rate. Derivatives are recorded at fair value, with changes in fair value taken to the income statement, except for cash flow hedging. Companies hedge against the many risks associated with financial instruments.

Non-current liabilities comprise borrowings and provisions. Borrowings include bank loans and debentures. They are usually secured, either by a fixed charge or by a floating charge. Most are redeemable. Compound financial instruments are required to be split into their component parts.

Provisions are liabilities of uncertain timing or amount. The most important are those for pensions and other employee benefits, and for restructuring. Estimating provisions poses difficult conceptual and practical problems.

The equity section of a consolidated balance sheet is divided between the equity attributable to the shareholders of the parent company and the minority interests. The former comprises share capital and reserves. Shareholders differ from debt holders in that they are members of the company not creditors, receive dividends not interest, and shares are not, except in special circumstances, redeemed. Ordinary shares, unlike preference shares, are not entitled to a fixed dividend, or to priority in a winding up. The par value of a share is not necessarily the same as its issue price (shares are often issued at a premium) or its market price. Dividends are paid by companies out of their retained earnings. The existence of reserves does not mean that a company has cash of an equal or greater amount.

The consolidated income statement is drawn up from the point of view of the shareholders. In it (or in the notes thereto) are disclosed items such as turnover (sales), cost of sales, gross profit, expenses, operating profit, profit before interest and taxation, interest, profit before taxation, taxation for the year, and profit after taxation.

Those items of income and expense which are not passed through the income statement are disclosed either in a consolidated statement of recognized income and expense (SORIE) or in a consolidated statement of changes in equity. The latter also records dividends.

The cash flow statement records cash inflows and outflows and demonstrates *inter alia* the difference between making profits and generating cash flows. A key figure is net cash from operating activities. It is net of interest paid and tax paid and is sometimes termed free cash flow. It is cash from operations available either for distribution to the shareholders or for investment. The cash flow statement also shows cash receipts and payments related to borrowings.

Most UK listed company groups have some subsidiaries whose financial statements are denominated in a currency other then sterling. These statements are in most cases incorporated in the consolidated statements by the closing rate method, whereby balance sheet items are translated at the closing rate of exchange and income statement items at the average rate for the accounting period.

A good introductory book on accounting is P. Weetman, *Financial Accounting: An Introduction* (Harlow: Financial Times Prentice Hall). There are many excellent guides to IFRS as applied in the UK. The standards themselves are published by LexisNexis on behalf of the IASB. The most detailed commentaries on them are written by those who have the greatest incentives and the most resources, viz, teams of experts from the international accountancy firms: Deloitte, *iGAAP 2007. IFRS Reporting in the UK* (Kingston upon Thames: Wolters Kluwer); Ernst & Young, *International GAAP 2007* (London: LexisNexis); KPMG International Financial Reporting Group, *Insights into IFRS* (London: Thomson); PricewaterhouseCoopers, *Manual of Accounting – IFRS in the UK* (Kingston upon Thames: CCH). These books are well-written but, given their great length, not for the faint-hearted. There is a less detailed commentary on IFRS in C. Nobes and R. Parker, *Comparative International Accounting* (Harlow: Financial Times Prentice Hall), which also looks at key issues in financial reporting and sets UK practice in its international context.

TAXATION

Chapter 3 dealt with taxation and audit. Companies pay corporation tax, not income tax. Taxable income is measured in a somewhat similar way to accounting profit, with the major exception of capital allowances (which replace depreciation). The corporation tax rate refers to a financial year which ends on 31 March, but companies are assessed on the basis of their own accounting periods. Companies collect on behalf of HM Revenue and Customs income tax deducted from the wages and salaries of their employees. They pay value added tax (VAT) on inputs and charge it on outputs.

Temporary differences between the balance sheet and the tax values of assets and liabilities taxable are treated as giving rise to taxation that has been deferred; the taxation charge in the income statement takes account of this. In the balance sheet the amounts for deferred tax liabilities and deferred tax assets can be significant.

Most books on taxation are written for accountants (lots of figures), lawyers (lots of case law) or economists (lots of diagrams). S. James and

C. Nobes, *The Economics of Taxation* (Harlow: Financial Times Prentice Hall) helpfully combines the perspectives of accounting and economics.

AUDIT

The main function of the auditor of a UK listed company is to give an opinion on whether the consolidated financial statements give a true and fair view in accordance with IFRS as adopted in the EU, and whether the parent company financial statements give a true and fair view either in accordance with UK GAAP or in accordance with IFRS as adopted in the EU. The opinion is addressed to the shareholders, and auditors are at pains to make it clear that they are not reporting to other interested stakeholders. There is an expectations gap between what auditors provide and what some stakeholders would like them to provide. Auditors must register with a recognized supervisory body (one of the professional accountancy bodies). They are supervised by the Professional Oversight Board, which is independent of the profession.

A useful textbook is B. Porter, J. Simon and D. Hatherly, *Principles of External Auditing* (Chichester: Wiley). The text of auditing standards is set out annually in *Accounting and Reporting* (London: Institute of Chartered Accountants in England and Wales). A discussion of how auditing can be improved can be found in W. M. McInnes, ed., *Auditing into the Twenty-first Century* (Edinburgh: Institute of Chartered Accountants of Scotland).

ACCOUNTING REGULATION AND ACCOUNTING CONCEPTS

Three sets of interrelated but different regulations apply to UK companies. The consolidated financial statements of listed companies must be prepared in accordance with IFRS as adopted by the EU. For all other statements there is a choice between IFRS and UK GAAP, with the proviso that those of companies below a certain size may be prepared in accordance with a simplified version of UK GAAP known as the FRSSE.

This position has evolved as a result of the globalization of world trade that led to the creation of an International Accounting Standards Committee (later Board), economic and political developments in the European Union, and the recognition that regulations appropriate to large listed companies are not necessarily suitable for all companies.

Financial reporting standards are set having regard to a conceptual framework developed by accountants but they are also influenced by political considerations. The directors of companies may lobby against rules that they dislike and indulge in creative accounting. Monitoring and enforcement is mainly through the activities of the Financial Reporting Review Panel, which has become more powerful and more active in recent years.

The IFRS books mentioned above all include material on the regulatory environment of financial reporting in the UK, as does the book by Nobes and Parker.

TOOLS OF ANALYSIS

Chapter 5 was concerned with defining and explaining the uses and limitations of ratios, percentages and yields as tools for the analysis of financial statements.

PROFITABILITY, RETURN ON INVESTMENT AND VALUE ADDED

Profitability, return on investment and value added were discussed in Chapter 6. Profitability relates profits to the investment made to generate them. Return on equity is the relationship between earnings after interest and tax to ordinary shareholders' equity. Return on assets relates profit (earnings) before interest and tax (EBIT) to total assets less current liabilities (equal in amount to shareholders' equity plus non-current liabilities).

Formats of the consolidated income statement vary but the major items can be compared over time and across companies both in absolute and percentage terms. Given the diversified nature of most listed companies, segmental analysis by line of business and geographically can be very revealing.

The data used in the income statement can be used to construct a value added statement although very few companies publish these in their annual reports. The emphasis is on gross value added (sales less bought-in goods and services) rather than any definition of profit.

LIQUIDITY AND CASH FLOWS

Chapter 7 stressed the necessity for a company to be liquid as well as profitable. Making profits is not the same as accumulating cash. It was shown that the best way to control liquidity from inside a company is by means of a cash budget. The external analyst uses rather cruder measures. These include the current ratio and the liquid ratio (both susceptible to window-dressing) and the defensive or no-credit interval.

Liquidity depends in part on how quickly debts are collected, bills paid and inventory turned over. These are measured by the average collection period, the average payment period and the average inventory turnover. The extreme case of illiquidity is insolvency; some success has been achieved in predicting this by means of financial ratios.

SOURCES OF FUNDS AND CAPITAL STRUCTURE

Chapter 8 discussed long-term sources of funds. These comprise shareholders' equity (share capital and reserves, including retained profits) and borrowings (debentures and other loans). The precise make-up differs from company to company.

The problem of capital structure is to obtain the best mix of debt and equity. Factors to be considered are cost, risk, control, acceptability and transferability. The earnings yield (reciprocal of the price–earnings ratio) and the dividend yield plus a growth rate are better measures of the cost of equity capital than the dividend yield itself. Calculations of earnings per share are complicated by dilution, exceptional items and the imputation system of corporate taxation.

Risk can be approached through traditional measures of gearing (leverage) or through the calculation of betas, which quantify the market risk of a share as distinct from its specific risk.

In deciding on a dividend policy, a company looks at its effect on the cost of capital, on dividend yield and on dividend cover and has to take account of government policy, inflation and taxation. A common policy is to pay a constant or steadily increasing dividend (in money terms), ironing out fluctuations in earnings, sometimes at the expense of dividend cover.

Rights issues give existing shareholders the first chance to subscribe to new issues. They are distinguished from bonus issues, where the existing shareholders receive extra shares without further subscription.

The many ways of raising funds include convertible loan stock, warrants and leasing. Some companies have tried to avoid putting debt in their balance sheets by ingenious means of off balance sheet financing. These attempts have been resisted by accounting standard-setters.

Books on the topics looked at in Chapter 5, 6, 7 and 8 are likely to have 'finance' rather than 'accounting' in their titles. Two well-established textbooks are R. A. Brealey and S. Myers, *Principles of Corporate Finance* (London: McGraw-Hill/Irwin) and J. M. Samuels, F. M. Wilkes and R. E. Brayshaw, *Financial Management and Decision Making* (London: International Thomson Business). Readers of the financial press should consult R. Vaitilingam, *The Financial Times Guide to Using the Financial Pages* (Harlow: Financial Times Prentice Hall).

Appendix A
Debits and Credits (Double Entry)

Welche Vorteile gewährt die doppelte Buchhaltung dem Kauf-
manne!
Johann Wolfgang von Goethe, *Wilhelm Meisters Lehrjahre*, I, x

Most people know that accountants are concerned with debits and
credits. Since it is possible to learn quite a lot about accounting and
finance without using these terms, it has not been thought necessary to
explain their meaning within the body of this book. Very little extra
effort is required, however, to understand the underlying principles of
double entry, so a brief explanation is given in this appendix.

It will be remembered from Chapter 2 that:

assets = liabilities + shareholders' equity

An increase on the left-hand side of this equation is called a debit
(abbreviated to Dr.), an increase on the right-hand side a credit (abbreviated to Cr.). Similarly, decreases on the left-hand side are credits, and
decreases on the right-hand side are debits. Debit and credit are used
here as technical terms and should not be confused with any other
meanings of these words.

It will also be remembered that shareholders' equity can be increased
by the retention of profits and that retained profits is equal to revenues
less expenses, tax and dividends. Since increases in retained profits are
credits, it follows that increases in revenues are also credits, whereas
increases in expenses, taxes and dividends must be debits. Conversely,
decreases in revenues are debits and decreases in expenses, taxes and
dividends are credits.

We can sum up the rules as follows:

DEBITS ARE		CREDITS ARE	
Increases in:	assets	Increases in:	liabilities
	expenses		share capital
	taxes		revenues
	dividends		
Decreases in:	liabilities	Decreases in:	assets
	share capital		expenses
	revenues		taxes
			dividends

It seems curious at first sight that both increases in assets and in expenses are debits. In fact, assets and expenses are much more closely linked than is usually realized. If a company buys for cash a machine which is expected to last ten years, it is rightly regarded as having acquired the asset machine (increase in machines, therefore debit 'machines') in exchange for the asset cash (decrease in cash, therefore credit 'cash'). Suppose, however, that technological change is so rapid that these machines have an economic life of only one year or less. Then, if the accounting period is one year, the machine can be regarded as an expense of the period (therefore, debit 'machine expense', credit 'cash'). Thus, in one sense, an asset is merely an expense paid for in advance which needs to be spread over several accounting periods in the form of depreciation.

The system of debits and credits is referred to as double entry, since maintenance of the accounting equation requires that any increase or decrease in one item be balanced by a corresponding increase or decrease in another item or items. There are always two sides to any transaction. Suppose, for example, that a company decreases its cash by £100. The other side of the transaction might be:

1. An increase in another asset such as a machine (so, debit 'machine', credit 'cash').
2. A decrease in a liability, such as a trade creditor (so, debit 'creditor', credit 'cash').
3. An increase in a negative shareholders' equity item such as expenses, taxes or dividends (so, debit 'expenses', 'taxes' or 'dividends', credit 'cash').

Note that cash is always credited (since the asset cash has been decreased) and that a negative credit is the same as a debit (and a negative debit the same as a credit).

Appendix B

Glossary of Accounting and Financial Terms

This glossary serves two purposes:

1. To collect in alphabetical order various definitions, descriptions and explanations scattered throughout the text.
2. To provide a limited amount of additional information.

Terms in SMALL CAPITALS are cross-references to other terms defined in the Glossary.

For definitions covering accounting and finance more generally, see C. Nobes, *The Penguin Dictionary of Accounting* (London: Penguin Books).

Abbreviated accounts. Financial statements in which advantage has been taken of the exemptions available to SMALL COMPANIES and MEDIUM-SIZED COMPANIES.

Accelerated depreciation. The writing off of the cost of an asset (e.g. for tax purposes) at a faster rate than is justified by the rate of use of the asset concerned.

Accounting identity (or equation.) Another name of the BALANCE SHEET IDENTITY.

Accounting period. The period between two balance sheets, usually a year from the point of view of shareholders and taxation authorities. Corporation tax is assessed on the basis of a company's accounting period.

Accounting policies. The accounting methods selected for use by a business enterprise in its financial statements. The choice is constrained by ACCOUNTING STANDARDS. Companies publish a list of accounting policies in their annual reports.

Accounting reference period. A company's ACCOUNTING PERIOD as notified to the REGISTRAR OF COMPANIES.

Accounting Regulatory Committee (ARC). A committee of government representatives from all member states of the European Union which considers whether to endorse or reject an international financial reporting standard for adoption within the EU.

Accounting standards. See FINANCIAL REPORTING STANDARDS, INTERNATIONAL FINANCIAL REPORTING STANDARDS.

Accounting Standards Board (ASB). The body prescribed in the UK under company law as a standard-setting body. It issues FINANCIAL REPORTING STANDARDS. Its standards do not apply to the consolidated financial statements of listed companies.

Accounting Standards Committee (ASC). The predecessor of the ACCOUNTING STANDARDS BOARD. It issued STATEMENTS OF STANDARD ACCOUNTING PRACTICE.

Accounts payable. Amounts owing by a company to suppliers.

Accounts receivable. Amounts owing to a company by customers.

Accrual basis of accounting. The accounting concept that revenues and expenses are recognized as they are earned or incurred, not as money is received or paid.

Accumulated depreciation. The cumulative amount of DEPRECIATION written off an asset at a balance sheet date.

Acid test. Another name for the LIQUID RATIO.

Allotment. The allocation of shares by the directors of a company following applications for them by intending shareholders.

Amortization. The writing off over a period of an asset (especially an INTANGIBLE ASSET) or a liability. Sometimes used synonymously with DEPRECIATION.

Annual general meeting (AGM). Meeting of the members (shareholders) of a company held annually. The usual business transacted includes reception of the directors' report and accounts; declaration of a dividend; election of directors; and appointment of auditors.

Annual report. Report made annually by the directors of a company to its shareholders. The contents are largely but not wholly determined by company law, financial reporting standards and other regulations.

Annual return. Document, available for public inspection, which all companies must file each year with the REGISTRAR OF COMPANIES, setting out information about the company, its members and directors. Copies of the directors' report, financial statements and auditors' report (to the extent that these are legal requirements for the particular company) must be annexed.

Applicable accounting standards. Accounting standards issued by a prescribed standard-setting body, such as the INTERNATIONAL ACCOUNTING STANDARDS BOARD or the ACCOUNTING STANDARDS BOARD.

Application money. The amount per share or unit of stock payable on application for a new issue of shares or DEBENTURES.

Articles of association. The internal regulations of a company. They deal with such matters as: rights of various classes of shares; calls on shares; transfer, transmission and forfeiture of shares; alteration of share capital; general meetings (notice, proceedings); votes and proxies; directors (powers, duties, disqualification, rotation, proceedings); dividends and reserves; accounts; capitalization of profits; audit; and winding-up.

Assets. Resources controlled by an enterprise as a result of past events and from which future economic benefits are expected to flow to the enterprise. Examples include PROPERTY, PLANT AND EQUIPMENT; copyrights; INVENTORIES; and cash.

Associate. An entity over which an investor has significant influence and which is neither a subsidiary nor an interest in a joint venture.

Audit committee. A committee which acts as a liaison between the board of directors and the AUDITORS. It usually has a majority of NON-EXECUTIVE DIRECTORS.

Audit expectations gap. The gap between what users expect from AUDITORS and what they think they are currently receiving.

Auditing Practices Board (APB). The body responsible for the issue of International Standards on Auditing (UK and Ireland) (a version of international auditing standards adapted for use in those countries).

Auditing standards. Standards issued by the AUDITING PRACTICES BOARD designed to give credibility to the independence and technical competence of AUDITORS.

Auditors. Independent experts who report to the shareholders of a company their opinion on the truth and fairness of published financial statements and whether they comply with APPLICABLE ACCOUNTING STANDARDS. Their remuneration must be disclosed, with separate disclosure of any non-audit services rendered. An auditor of a company must be a REGISTERED AUDITOR and a member of a RECOGNIZED SUPERVISORY BODY. The auditor must not be an officer or servant (or an employee thereof) of the company or of a company in the same group.

Average collection period. The average time in days that a company takes to collect its ACCOUNTS RECEIVABLE.

Average payment period. The average time in days that a company takes to settle its ACCOUNTS PAYABLE.

Bad debt. An amount owing to a company which is not expected to be received. It is written off either directly to the INCOME STATEMENT or by way of a previously established allowance for bad (or doubtful) debts.

Balanced scorecard. A reporting technique that gives equal weight to financial and non-financial measures of performance.

Balance sheet. A statement of the assets, liabilities and shareholders' equity of an enterprise at a particular date.

Balance sheet identity (or equation). The identity: assets *equals* liabilities *plus* shareholders' equity.

Bearer securities. DEBENTURES or shares that are not registered and are transferable by simple delivery.

Beta. A measure of the market (or systematic) risk of a company's shares (i.e. the sensitivity of the share price to movements in the market).

Big Four. The four largest public accountancy firms worldwide.

Bonds. Fixed interest securities such as company or government loans.

Bonus shares. Shares issued to existing shareholders without further payment on their part. Also referred to as a capitalization issue, a scrip issue, or (in the USA) a stock dividend.

Book value. The monetary value of an item in the balance sheet or in the accounting records (books of account).

Brand. A means of distinguishing a product or service (or sometimes its manufacturer or distributor) from its competitors. Usually treated as an INTANGIBLE ASSET with an indefinite life and subject to IMPAIRMENT but not systematic AMORTIZATION.

Called-up share capital. The amount of the ISSUED SHARE CAPITAL which has been called up (i.e. the amount that shareholders have been asked to pay to date). Equal to the PAID-UP SHARE CAPITAL unless there are CALLS in arrears or calls that have been paid in advance.

Calls. Demands by a company for part or all of the balance owing on partly-paid shares.

Capital allowance. In effect, the DEPRECIATION allowance for tax purposes. It can differ substantially from the depreciation charged in the financial statements.

Capital asset pricing model (CAPM). A model of the securities market based on PORTFOLIO analysis. According to the CAPM the expected return in equilibrium of any risky asset in a perfect capital market is a function of the expected rate of return for the MARKET PORTFOLIO, the risk-free rate of return, and the SYSTEMATIC RISK of the asset (BETA).

Capital employed. Usually refers to the total of shareholders' equity plus non-current liabilities (equal in amount to non-current assets plus current assets net of current liabilities).

Capital expenditure. Expenditure on non-current assets.

Capital gain. A gain resulting not from operations but from the holding of an asset.

Capital gains tax. A tax levied on individuals on gains realized on the disposal of assets. Companies pay CORPORATION TAX on their capital gains.

Capitalization issue. *See* BONUS SHARES.

Capitalize. To recognize an asset in the accounting records and in a balance sheet.

Capital redemption reserve. When shares are redeemed otherwise than out of a new issue of shares, a sum equal to their nominal value must be transferred out of retained earnings to an account with this name. For most purposes this reserve is treated as if it were share capital.

Capital structure. The composition of a company's sources of funds, especially long-term.

Cash budget. A plan of future cash receipts and payments based on specified assumptions concerning sales growth, credit terms, etc.

Cash flow. The flows of cash into and out of a company.

Cash flow statement. A statement showing a company's inflows and outflows of cash during an accounting period.

Cash generating unit. The smallest group of assets for which cash inflows and outflows can be separately identified. IMPAIRMENT is measured with respect to cash generating units.

CESR. *See* COMMITTEE OF EUROPEAN SECURITIES REGULATORS.

Chairman's review (or statement). Statement made by the chairman of a company at its annual general meeting and often included in the annual report. There are no regulations as to its content but it often contains interesting and useful information.

CIC. Community interest company.

Close company. A company resident in the UK which is under the control of five or fewer participators, or of participators who are directors.

Combined Code. A voluntary code on CORPORATE GOVERNANCE which is the responsibility of the FINANCIAL REPORTING COUNCIL. It is backed by the UK Listing Authority and operates on a comply or explain basis. Compliance with the Code is reviewed by the auditors.

Committee of European Securities Regulators (CESR). A committee of the national regulatory bodies responsible for regulating securities markets within Europe. The UK representative is the FINANCIAL SERVICES AUTHORITY (FSA).

Common stock. US term for ordinary shares.

Company. Refers mainly to corporate bodies registered under the Companies Act. The liability of the members of most companies is limited, either by shares or by guarantee. *See* LISTED COMPANY, PRIVATE COMPANY, PUBLIC COMPANY.

Conceptual framework. A set of interrelated concepts underlying the procedures of financial reporting. That issued by the INTERNATIONAL ACCOUNTING STANDARDS BOARD is entitled *Framework for the Preparation and Presentation of Financial Statements.*

Conservatism. *See* PRUDENCE.

Consolidated balance sheet. Balance sheet of a group of companies as distinct from that of an individual company (e.g. the parent company of the group).

Consolidated income statement. Income statement of a group of companies as distinct from that of the parent company only.

Contingent asset. A possible asset that arises from past events and whose existence will be confirmed only by the occurrence or non-occurrence of one or more uncertain future events not wholly within the control of the company.

Contingent liability. A possible obligation that arises from past events and whose existence will be confirmed only by the occurrence or non-occurrence of one or more uncertain events that are not wholly within the control of the company. Also, a present obligation that arises from past events where it is not probable that an outflow of resources will be required, or where the amount of the obligation cannot be measured with sufficient reliability.

Convertible loan stock. Loan stock which may be converted at the option of the holder at a future date or dates into ordinary shares.

Corporate governance. The processes by which companies are governed, including the relationships between shareholders, directors (executive and non-executive), third parties (e.g. creditors) and auditors, and the regulation of companies by the state. *See also* COMBINED CODE.

Corporate social responsibility report. A report by a company dealing with social and environmental rather than financial information and addressed to all users not just shareholders. The content is not regulated and not always published as part of the annual report. It typically refers to matters such as employment, the environment, and health and safety.

Corporation tax. A tax on the profits of companies, not individuals. There is a lower rate for small profits.

Cost of capital. The cost to a company of obtaining funds for investment.

Cost of sales. The cost of goods sold during a period, calculated by adjusting cost of goods purchased or manufactured by the change in inventories.

Coupon rate of interest. The rate of interest on the PAR VALUE of a debenture or bond. Not necessarily equal to the EFFECTIVE RATE.

Creative accounting. The use of accounting to mislead rather than help the intended user. *See also* OFF BALANCE SHEET FINANCING, WINDOW-DRESSING.

Credit. *See* DOUBLE ENTRY.

Creditors. Amounts owed by a company to suppliers. Also called accounts payable.

Cumulative preference shares. PREFERENCE SHARES entitled to be paid the amount of their dividend before any dividend is paid on the ordinary shares. Any arrears must be disclosed.

Current assets. Those assets expected to be realized, sold, or consumed within one year or within a company's normal operating cycle. Examples include inventories, accounts receivable and cash.

Current liabilities. Those liabilities that will have to be settled within one year or within a company's normal operating cycle. Examples include accounts payable and current taxation.

Current ratio. Ratio of current assets to current liabilities. A measure of liquidity.

Current taxation. Tax payable relating to the current accounting period.

Debenture discount. Arises from issuing debentures at less than their par value. Disclosed in the notes to the extent that it has not been written off.

Debentures. Loans, usually, but not necessarily, secured on the assets of the company. Usually redeemable but may be irredeemable.

Debit. *See* DOUBLE ENTRY.

Debtors. Amounts owing to a company from customers. Also called accounts receivable.

Defensive interval. A measure of how many days operating expense can be paid out of a company's LIQUID ASSETS.

Deferred taxation. Taxation implied by TEMPORARY DIFFERENCES between accounting and tax measures of balance sheet items. Such amounts can be either a liability or an asset. The tax rate used is generally that at the date of the balance sheet.

Depreciation. The systematic allocation of the cost or revalued amount (net of estimated residual value) of a tangible non-current asset over its useful life. Annual depreciation is charged in the income statement. Accumulated depreciation is deducted from the cost or revalued amount of the asset in the balance sheet.

Derivatives. FINANCIAL ASSETS or LIABILITIES, such as OPTIONS and futures, that derive their value from an underlying security or commodity.

Dilution. The decrease in control and/or EARNINGS PER SHARE suffered by existing shareholders when a new issue of shares is wholly or partly subscribed to by new shareholders.

Directive. Within the European Union, a statement adopted by the Council of Ministers and the European Parliament on the proposal of the European Commission. Directives are implemented through national legislation.

Directors' remuneration report. A report, required by company law, setting out in detail the remuneration of the directors, including salaries, fees, pensions, share-based payments and compensation for loss of office. Parts of it are required to be audited. *See* REMUNERATION COMMITTEE.

Directors' report. Report required by company law to be made annually to shareholders by the board of directors. The items which must be reported relate *inter alia* to principal activities, dividends, employees and directors.

Discounting. Reducing the value of expected future cash receipts and payments by taking account of the time value of money.

Distributable reserves. A company's accumulated realized profits so far as not previously distributed or capitalized, less its accumulated realized losses so far as not previously written off in a reduction or reorganization of share capital. Public companies may pay a dividend only if the net assets are not less than the aggregate of the called-up share capital and the undistributed reserves. The financial statements used to ascertain these amounts are those of an individual company *not* the consolidated statements of a group of companies.

Dividend. That part of a company's DISTRIBUTABLE RESERVES which is distributed to the shareholders. May be interim (paid during the financial year) or final (recommended by the directors for approval by the shareholders at the annual general meeting).

Dividend cover. The ratio between EARNINGS PER SHARE and the ordinary dividend per share.

Dividend policy. A company's policy on how to divide its profits between distributions to shareholders (dividends) and reinvestment (retained profits).

Dividend yield. The ratio between the ordinary dividend and the market price per ordinary share.

Double entry. A system of recording transactions in 'debits' and 'credits' based on the BALANCE SHEET IDENTITY. Broadly, increases in assets and decreases in liabilities and equity items (including expenses) are debits, and increases in liabilities and equity items (including revenues) and decreases in assets are credits.

Doubtful debt. Amount owing to a company that it is doubtful of receiving. It is usual to establish an allowance for doubtful debts so that ACCOUNTS RECEIVABLE are not overstated in the balance sheet.

Earnings per share (EPS). Profit attributable to the ordinary share-holders (after deduction of interest, tax and preference share dividends) divided by the weighted average number of ordinary shares. May be calculated on a NET or NIL BASIS. 'Basic EPS' is supplemented by 'diluted EPS' to take account of share options and convertible loan stock. Companies often also report a 'headline EPS' based on earnings exclusive of exceptional items and discontinued operations.

Earnings yield. The relationship between EPS and the market price per ordinary share. The reciprocal of the PRICE–EARNINGS RATIO multiplied by 100.

EBIT. Earnings before interest and tax.

EBITDA. Earnings before interest, tax, depreciation and amortization.

Effective rate of interest. The rate of interest on the market price of a debenture or bond. Not necessarily equal to the COUPON RATE OF INTEREST.

Employee report. A corporate financial report addressed to employees, published either separately or as a supplement to a house magazine. Usually also available to shareholders and other interested parties. May include a VALUE ADDED STATEMENT.

Equity instrument. A contract giving a right to a residual interest in the assets of an enterprise after deduction of all liabilities. Ordinary shares are the most common example.

Equity method. Method of accounting for investments in ASSOCIATES. Also known as one-line consolidation.

Equity shares. The ordinary shares of a company.

European Financial Reporting Advisory Group (EFRAG). A private-sector committee of accountants drawn from member states of the EU which advises the ACCOUNTING REGULATORY COMMITTEE.

Ex. Latin for 'without'. A price so quoted excludes any dividend (div.), bonus issue, rights or other distribution.

Exceptional items. Items which companies consider to be exceptional on account of size and/or incidence, which derive from the ordinary activities of an enterprise, and which are disclosed because of their size or incidence. Although used in practice, the term is not found in IFRS. Compare EXTRAORDINARY ITEMS.

Executive director. A director of a company who is involved in its day-to-day operations.

Extraordinary items. Material items which companies consider to possess a high degree of abnormality and which arise from events or transactions that fall outside the ordinary activities of a company and are expected not to recur. This concept is banned by IFRS. Compare EXCEPTIONAL ITEMS.

Fair value. The amount for which an asset could be exchanged, or a liability settled, between knowledgeable and willing parties at arm's length. It is calculated before the addition or subtraction of any buying or selling costs.

Finance lease. A LEASE that transfers substantially all the risks and rewards of ownership to the lessee. Both the leased asset and the liability to pay future lease rentals are shown in the balance sheet.

Financial assets. Cash, ACCOUNTS RECEIVABLE and INVESTMENTS.

Financial instrument. Any contract that gives rise to a FINANCIAL ASSET of one entity and a FINANCIAL LIABILITY or EQUITY INSTRUMENT of another entity.

Financial liability. Any liability that is a contractual obligation to deliver cash or another financial asset to another enterprise, or to exchange financial instruments with another enterprise under conditions that are potentially unfavourable.

Financial Reporting Council (FRC). The body that appoints the members of, and raises the funds for, the ACCOUNTING STANDARDS BOARD, the AUDITING PRACTICES BOARD, the FINANCIAL REPORTING REVIEW PANEL, and the PROFESSIONAL OVERSIGHT BOARD FOR ACCOUNTANCY.

Financial Reporting Review Panel (FRRP). A panel that monitors the compliance of companies with FINANCIAL REPORTING STANDARDS. It has the power to apply to the court to enforce its findings.

Financial reporting standards. Standards issued by the INTERNATIONAL FINANCIAL REPORTING STANDARDS BOARD (IFRS) and the ACCOUNTING STANDARDS BOARD (FRS).

Financial Services Authority (FSA). The government agency responsible, *inter alia*, for the supervision of the securities markets.

Financial statements. Statements such as those showing financial position (balance sheet), gains and losses for a period (income statement, statement of recognized income and expense, SORIE) and cash flows for a period (cash flow statement). Some companies publish a statement of changes in equity instead of a SORIE.

Financial year. The period for which an ANNUAL REPORT is prepared. The most popular period for UK companies is 1 January to 31 December. For corporation tax purposes the year runs from 1 April to the following 31 March.

Fixed assets. Another term for NON-CURRENT ASSETS.

Fixed charge. The right of a creditor to the proceeds from the sale of a specific asset or assets if the debtor does not pay an amount when due. Compare FLOATING CHARGE.

Flat yield. A YIELD which does not take account of the redemption value of a security.

Floating charge. The right of a creditor to the proceeds from the sale of all or a class of assets (e.g. inventories) if the debtor does not pay an amount when due. Unlike a FIXED CHARGE, the debtor is entitled to sell the assets until default.

Foreign currency translation. The translation of foreign currency transactions or of the financial statements of foreign subsidiaries into a company's reporting currency.

Foreign currency translation reserve. A RESERVE to which are credited and debited gains and losses recorded on the translation of balance sheet and income statement items expressed in foreign currencies.

Format. The method of presentation of a financial statement.

Free cash flow. Cash flow generated from operations after deduction of taxation and interest payments.

FRSSE. Financial Reporting Standard for Smaller Entities. The only reporting standard that small entities (including small companies) are required to comply with.

Functional currency. The currency in which a company operates on a day-to-day basis and in which it generates net cash flows. Usually, but not always, the currency of the country in which the company is located.

GAAP. US acronym for GENERALLY ACCEPTED ACCOUNTING PRINCIPLES. Outside the US used as an acronym for GENERALLY ACCEPTED ACCOUNTING PRACTICE. *See* INTERNATIONAL GAAP, UK GAAP.

Gearing. The relationship, measured in either balance sheet or income statement terms, between the funds provided to a company by equity holders and the funds provided by debt holders. Also known as leverage.

Generally accepted accounting practice. General term for the financial reporting rules applicable to non-US companies subject to international and/or national FINANCIAL REPORTING STANDARDS.

Generally accepted accounting principles. The financial reporting regulations applicable in the US to companies required to register with the Securities and Exchange Commission.

Going concern. An accounting concept that assumes that an enterprise will continue in operational existence for the foreseeable future.

Goodwill. The difference between the value of a company as a whole and the sum of the fair values of the tangible and identifiable intangible assets net of liabilities and contingent liabilities.

Goodwill on consolidation. The excess at the date of acquisition of the cost of shares in subsidiaries or associates or joint ventures over the fair values of their tangible and identifiable intangible assets net of liabilities and contingent liabilities. The carrying amount of goodwill on consolidation is tested at least annually for impairment. It can only appear in a consolidated balance sheet.

Green reporting. The reporting of information, both quantitative and qualitative, of a company's impact on the environment.

Gross profit. The excess of sales over cost of sales.

Guarantee, company limited by. A company the liability of whose members is limited to contributing a predetermined amount in the event of the company being wound up.

Harmonization. The process of narrowing differences in accounting rules and practices, especially among countries.

Headline earnings per share. A measure of EARNINGS PER SHARE before items claimed to be non-recurring.

Hedge accounting. Offsetting, for accounting purposes, changes in the fair values or cash flows of a HEDGED ITEM by those of a HEDGING INSTRUMENT.

Hedged item. An item exposed to the risk of changes in fair value or in future cash flows and offset by a HEDGING INSTRUMENT.

Hedging instrument. An asset or a liability, changes in the fair value of which or in the cash flows generated by it, are expected to offset changes in the fair value or cash flows of a HEDGED ITEM.

Historical cost. The monetary amount for which an asset was originally purchased or produced. Usually provides RELIABLE though not always RELEVANT INFORMATION.

IASB. *See* INTERNATIONAL ACCOUNTING STANDARDS BOARD.

IASC. *See* INTERNATIONAL ACCOUNTING STANDARDS COMMITTEE.

IFRS. *See* INTERNATIONAL FINANCIAL REPORTING STANDARDS.

Impairment. A loss in value of an asset below its depreciated cost. An impairment loss is an expense in the income statement.

Imputation system. System of corporate taxation under which, as used in the UK, all or part of the tax paid on distributed profits by the company is credited to the shareholders, thus mitigating double taxation.

Income statement. Statement of the revenues, expenses and profits of a company for a specified period.

Income tax. A tax on individuals; not payable by companies. Rates of income tax vary over time.

Industry ratio. An average ratio for an industry.

Inflation accounting. System of accounting that allows for changes in general and/or specific prices.

Insolvency. An inability to pay debts as they fall due.

Institutional shareholders. Shareholders, particularly insurance companies and investment funds, other than persons, industrial and commercial companies, the public sector and overseas investors.

Intangible assets. Non-monetary assets such as GOODWILL, BRANDS, patents, trademarks, copyright and software which have no tangible form.

Interim dividend. *See* DIVIDEND.

Interim report. Report issued by a company to its shareholders during a financial year (e.g. half-yearly, quarterly).

Internal control. The whole system of controls, financial and otherwise, established by a company's management in order to carry on the business in an orderly and efficient manner, ensure adherence to management policies, safeguard the assets, and secure the accuracy and completeness of the records.

International accounting standards (IAS). The standards issued by the former INTERNATIONAL ACCOUNTING STANDARDS COMMITTEE. They are gradually being replaced by INTERNATIONAL FINANCIAL REPORTING STANDARDS.

International Accounting Standards Board (IASB). The independent body, based in London, which issues INTERNATIONAL FINANCIAL REPORTING STANDARDS.

International Auditing and Assurance Standards Board (IAASB). A committee of the INTERNATIONAL FEDERATION OF ACCOUNTANTS responsible for the issue of INTERNATIONAL STANDARDS ON AUDITING.

International auditing standards. *See* INTERNATIONAL STANDARDS ON AUDITING.

International Federation of Accountants (IFAC). A body, based in New York, composed of representatives of all the world's major accountancy bodies. A committee of IFAC issues international auditing standards but IFAC is not responsible for international financial reporting standards.

International Financial Reporting Interpretations Committee (IFRIC). A body set up by the INTERNATIONAL ACCOUNTING STANDARDS BOARD to issue interpretations of IFRS.

International financial reporting standards (IFRS). The standards issued by the INTERNATIONAL ACCOUNTING STANDARDS BOARD. Compulsory for the consolidated financial statements of UK listed companies and permitted for all other UK company financial statements.

International GAAP. The financial reporting rules set out in IFRS and the interpretations thereof issued by the International Financial Reporting Interpretations Committee of the IASB.

International Organization of Securities Commissions (IOSCO). An international organization of stock exchange regulators, including the Financial Services Authority in the UK and the Securities and Exchange Commission in the US. IOSCO has recommended its members to accept IFRS for foreign issuers.

International standards on auditing (ISAs). The standards issued by the INTERNATIONAL AUDITING AND ASSURANCE STANDARDS BOARD. A local version has been adopted for the UK and Ireland by the AUDITING PRACTICES BOARD.

Inventories. General term for: goods or other assets purchased for resale; consumable stores; raw material and components; WORK IN PROGRESS; and finished goods. Usually valued at the lower of cost and NET REALIZABLE VALUE.

Inventory turnover. Ratio of cost of sales to inventories.

Investment property. Property held by the owner or on a finance lease to earn rentals or for capital appreciation or both, rather than for use in supplying goods or services or for administrative purposes, or for sale in the ordinary course of business.

Investments. FINANCIAL ASSETS other than cash and ACCOUNTS RECEIVABLE. Investments are categorized as held for trading, held to maturity, available for sale, and loans and receivables.

Investment trust. Not a trust but a company whose object is investment in the securities of other companies. Compare UNIT TRUST.

Irredeemable debenture. A DEBENTURE that will never have to be repaid.

Issued share capital. The amount of share capital that has been issued to members of the company. It is not necessarily equal to the CALLED-UP SHARE CAPITAL or the PAID-UP SHARE CAPITAL.

Issue expenses. Expenses of making an issue of shares or debentures.

Issue price. The price at which a share or debenture is issued; not necessarily equal to the PAR VALUE.

Joint venture. A contractual arrangement whereby two or more parties undertake an activity that is subject to joint control.

Leasing. Entering into a contract which allows the use of an asset in return for a periodic rental, but does not usually give ownership. A distinction is made between a FINANCE LEASE and an OPERATING LEASE.

Leverage. US term for GEARING.

Liabilities. The present obligations of an enterprise, arising from past events, the settlement of which is expected to result in an outflow from the enterprise of resources embodying economic benefits. Examples include ACCOUNTS PAYABLE, loans and DEBENTURES.

Limited liability company. A company the liability of whose members is limited by shares or by guarantee. If by shares, liability is limited to the amount taken or agreed to be taken up; if by guarantee, to the amount undertaken to be contributed in the event of winding up.

Limited liability partnership (LLP). A partnership (not a company), the liability of whose partners is limited. Unlike other partnerships, an LLP is required to publish audited financial statements.

Liquid assets. Current assets excluding inventories.

Liquid ratio. The relationship between liquid assets and current liabilities. Also known as the quick ratio, or the acid test.

Listed company. A company whose shares or debentures are listed (quoted) on a stock exchange.

Loan capital. Funds acquired by borrowing from sources other than the shareholders of a company.

Long-term debt. Long-term sources of funds other than equity (share capital and reserves).

Market capitalization. The total value on a stock exchange of a listed company's shares.

Market portfolio. A PORTFOLIO of all the securities traded on a securities market.

Market price. The price at which a company's shares can be bought and sold on a stock exchange.

Marking to market. Valuing an asset at its FAIR VALUE and taking any resultant gains and losses to the income statement.

Materiality. An accounting concept that requires disclosure only of data that are significant enough to be relevant to the needs of the potential user of a financial statement.

Medium-sized companies. PRIVATE COMPANIES with the privilege of filing abbreviated income statements with the Registrar of Companies. 'Medium' is measured in terms of total assets, turnover and average number of employees.

Medium-sized groups. *See* SMALL AND MEDIUM-SIZED GROUPS.

Memorandum of association. A memorandum stating that the subscribers to it wish to form a company under the Companies Act, agree to become members of it, and to subscribe to at least one share (if the company is to have a share capital).

Minority interest. That part of a subsidiary company's shareholders' equity that is not held by the parent company.

Monetary assets. Assets (e.g. cash, accounts receivable) that have a fixed monetary exchange value that is not affected by a change in the general price level.

Net basis. Method of calculating EARNINGS PER SHARE which takes account of both constant and variable components in the tax charge.

Net debt. Loans and other borrowings, both current and non-current, net of cash and cash equivalents.

Net profit. The excess of revenues over expenses. Calculated before or after exceptional items, and before or after tax, depending on the context.

Net profit ratio. Ratio of net profit to sales.

Net realizable value. The amount for which an asset can be sold, net of the expenses of completion and of sale.

Nil basis. Method of calculating EARNINGS PER SHARE which assumes a nil distribution of dividends.

No-credit interval. Alternative term for DEFENSIVE INTERVAL.

Nominee shareholder. A shareholder who holds shares on behalf of another person or company (the beneficial shareholder).

Non-current assets. All assets that are not CURRENT ASSETS. They are intended for use on a continuing basis and include PROPERTY, PLANT AND EQUIPMENT; INTANGIBLE ASSETS; and FINANCIAL ASSETS.

Non-current liabilities. Those liabilities that do not have to be settled within one year or within a company's normal operating cycle.

Non-executive directors. Directors who take no part in the day-to-day operations of a company.

Non-monetary assets. Assets other than monetary assets, e.g. property, plant and equipment; brands; inventories.

Non-voting shares. Shares with no voting rights. Often called 'A' shares, they are usually cheaper to buy than those with votes.

Notes to the financial statement. Notes attached to, and explanatory of, the items in the financial statements. They may be very detailed.

Off balance sheet financing. Financing assets by 'borrowing' in such a fashion that the debt does not appear in the balance sheet.

Operating and financial review. An analysis and explanation in narrative form of the main features of a company's performance and financial position.

Operating lease. A LEASE that does not transfer substantially all the risks and rewards of ownership to the lessee. The annual lease rentals are an expense in the income statement and the total commitments are disclosed in the notes.

Operating profit. The excess of operating revenues over operating expenses.

Ordinary shareholders. Members of a company who are entitled to share the profits after payment of loan interest and preference dividends.

Overtrading. A situation in which a company expands its sales and may appear to be highly profitable but does not have the resources available to finance the expansion and is therefore in danger of running out of cash.

Paid-up share capital. The amount of the CALLED-UP SHARE CAPITAL which has been paid up by the shareholders.

Parent company. A company that has one or more SUBSIDIARY COMPANIES. A parent company (except that of a SMALL OR MEDIUM-SIZED GROUP) must prepare and publish consolidated as well as individual company financial statements.

Par value. The face or nominal value of a share or debenture. Not necessarily equal to the ISSUE PRICE or the current MARKET PRICE. Dividend and interest percentages refer to the par value, YIELDS to the current market price.

Portfolio. A collection of securities that can be evaluated in terms of their combined risks and returns.

Post balance sheet events. Events occurring after the date of the balance sheet. They are either 'adjusting events' (those providing additional evidence of conditions existing at the balance sheet date) or 'non-adjusting events'.

Pre-emption right. The entitlement of an existing shareholder to an allotment of a proportionate part of a new issue of shares.

Preference shares. Shares which are usually entitled to a fixed rate of dividend before a dividend is paid on the ordinary shares, and to priority of repayment if the company is wound up. Participating preference shares are also entitled to a further dividend if profits are available. If a preference dividend is not paid, the arrears must be disclosed in the notes. Arrears can only arise if the shares are cumulative as distinct from non-cumulative.

Preliminary announcement. An announcement of annual results, obligatory for listed companies, made by the directors before the full audited results are published.

Preliminary expenses. Expenses of forming a company.

Price–earnings ratio. The current market price of one ordinary share divided by the last reported EARNINGS PER SHARE. This shows the multiple of the EPS that the market is willing to pay for one ordinary share. It is equal to the reciprocal of the EARNINGS YIELD multiplied by 100.

Prior charges. Claims on a company's assets and profits that rank ahead of ordinary share capital.

Priority percentages. Method of calculating GEARING by computing the percentage of earnings that is required to service each category of loan and share capital.

Prior year adjustments. Material adjustments applicable to prior years arising from changes in ACCOUNTING POLICIES or the correction of errors.

Private company. A company which is not a PUBLIC LIMITED COMPANY. Not permitted to issue shares or debentures to the public. Its name must end in 'Limited' or 'Ltd' ('cyf' for Welsh companies).

Professional Oversight Board (POB). A body, independent of the profession and responsible to the FINANCIAL REPORTING COUNCIL, which oversees the regulation of auditors by the RECOGNIZED SUPERVISORY BODIES (i.e. the major professional accountancy bodies), and monitors the quality of audits of economically significant entities.

Profit. A general term for the excess of revenues over expenses.

Profit and loss account. Alternative term for INCOME STATEMENT.

Property, plant and equipment. Tangible assets held by an enterprise for use in the production or supply of goods and services, for rental to others or for administrative purposes, and which are expected to be used during more than one accounting period.

Prospectus. Any notice, circular, advertisement or other invitation offering shares or debentures to the public.

Provision. A LIABILITY that is uncertain in timing or amount. Examples are provisions for pensions and for restructuring. Provisions are recognized in a balance sheet only if there is a present obligation that can be reliably measured (hence neither proposed final dividends nor CONTINGENT LIABILITIES are provisions).

Proxy. A person appointed to attend and vote at a company meeting on behalf of a shareholder, or the form, signed by the shareholder, which grants that authority.

Prudence. Accounting concept under which revenue and profits are not anticipated but are recognized for inclusion in the INCOME STATE-

MENT only when realized in cash or other assets the ultimate realization of which can be assessed with reasonable certainty. PROVISIONS are made for all known liabilities.

Public limited company. A company whose certificate of incorporation states that it is a public company, whose name ends with the words 'public limited company' (plc; ccc for Welsh companies) and which has a minimum allotted share capital of £50,000. Unlike a PRIVATE LIMITED COMPANY, a plc is permitted (but not required) to issue shares or debentures to the public.

Quick assets. Current assets less inventories.

Quick ratio. *See* LIQUID RATIO.

Quoted company. A company whose shares or debentures are quoted (listed) on a stock exchange.

Recognition criteria. The criteria (probable future economic benefits and reliable measurement) which items complying with the definitions of ASSETS and LIABILITIES must meet in order to be included in balance sheets.

Recognized supervisory body. An accountancy body recognized for the purpose of overseeing and maintaining the conduct and technical standards of company AUDITORS.

Recoverable amount. The greater of the FAIR VALUE (less costs to sell) of an asset or cash-generating unit and its VALUE IN USE.

Redeemable shares. Shares which must or may be redeemed at the option of the company or (very rarely) the shareholder.

Redemption yield. A YIELD which takes into account not only the annual interest receivable but also the redemption value of a security.

Registered auditor. A person or firm whose name is inscribed on a statutory register as qualified for appointment as a company AUDITOR.

Registered office. The official address of a company.

Registrar of Companies. Government agency with whom annual reports (including financial statements where required) and other company documents must be filed; in Cardiff for companies registered in England and Wales, in Edinburgh for companies registered in Scotland, in Belfast for companies registered in Northern Ireland.

Relevant information. Information that is timely and that has either predictive value (is useful in predicting future accounting numbers) or feedback value (is capable of confirming or correcting expectations).

Reliable information. Information that is verifiable and neutral.

Remuneration committee. A committee of non-executive directors of a listed company responsible for approving directors' remuneration and the contents of the DIRECTORS' REMUNERATION REPORT.

Research and development costs. Expenditure on research and development. Research costs are never recognized as assets; in limited circumstances development costs are recognized as amortizable intangible assets.

Reserve. Non-distributed gains arising either from the retention of profits or from events such as the issue of shares at a premium or the revaluation of assets. Not usually represented by cash on the other side of the balance sheet equation. Movements in reserves must be disclosed.

Reserve fund. A RESERVE which is represented by specially ear-marked cash or other financial assets.

Retained profits. Profits not distributed to shareholders but reinvested in the company. Their cost as a source of capital is less than that of a new issue of shares because of the issue costs of the latter.

Return on assets. The ratio of profit (earnings) before interest and tax (EBIT) to total assets less current liabilities (equal in amount to shareholders' equity plus non-current liabilities).

Return on equity. The ratio of earnings after interest and tax to ordinary shareholders' equity.

Revaluation. The writing up of the value of an asset in a balance sheet.

Revaluation reserve. The amount of gain or loss, not yet written off, arising from the revaluation of an asset.

Revenue expenditure. Expenditure that is written off completely in the INCOME STATEMENT in the accounting period in which it is incurred.

Reverse yield gap. The excess of the average yield on government bonds over the average dividend yield on the ordinary shares of listed companies, despite the greater monetary security of the former.

Rights issue. An issue of shares in which the existing shareholders have a right to subscribe for the new shares at a stated price. The right can be sold if the shareholder does not wish to subscribe.

Risk. *See* SYSTEMATIC RISK and SPECIFIC RISK.

Sale and lease back. Raising cash by selling an asset and then leasing it back in a long-term contract. *See* LEASING.

Scrip issue. *See* BONUS SHARES.

Securities. A generic name for stocks, shares, debentures, etc.

Securities and Exchange Commission (SEC). US federal agency responsible for the regulation of the securities markets, including, *inter alia*, the enforcement of accounting standards. It has the right, which it has largely allowed the Financial Accounting Standards Board to exercise, to establish accounting principles.

Security. The backing for a loan.

Segment reporting. Reporting items (e.g. sales, results, assets) of a diversified group of companies by major lines of business and by geographical area.

Share-based payments. Payments to employees (and others) in shares or in assets related to share prices. In most cases, they are accounted for both as an expense in the income statement and an increase in equity in the balance sheet.

Share capital. Shareholders' equity contributed by the owners of a company. Unless limited by guarantee, a company registered under the Companies Acts must have a capital divided into shares of a fixed amount. The ownership of a share gives a shareholder a proportionate ownership of the company. The share capital is stated in the balance sheet at its par (nominal) value.

Shareholder. A member of a company, the ownership of which is divided into shares.

Shareholders' equity. The proprietorship section of a company balance sheet. Includes the SHARE CAPITAL and the RESERVES.

Shareholders' funds. Alternative term for SHAREHOLDERS' EQUITY.

Share option. The right to buy or sell shares at a stated price within a stated period.

Share premium. The excess over the PAR VALUE on an issue of shares. Cannot be used to pay dividends but can be used to make an issue of BONUS SHARES.

Simplified financial statements. Financial statements prepared so that those unskilled in accounting may more readily understand them. *See also* SUMMARY FINANCIAL STATEMENTS.

Sinking fund. A fund established to accumulate the amount of money required to pay off a debt at a set date in the future.

Small and medium-sized groups. Groups of companies which are exempt from filing consolidated financial statements with the Registrar of Companies. 'Small' and 'medium' are measured in terms of turnover, balance sheet total and average number of employees.

Small companies. PRIVATE COMPANIES with the privilege of filing an abbreviated balance sheet and not filing an income statement and directors' report. 'Small' is measured in terms of turnover, balance sheet total and average number of employees. Depending on the size of their turnover and balance sheet total, many private companies are not required to be audited.

Small companies rate. A reduced rate of corporation tax paid by companies with small taxable incomes. This tax relief is not related to SMALL COMPANIES as defined in the Companies Act.

Solvency. The ability of a debtor to pay debts as they fall due.

Specific risk. Risk arising from factors specific to a company and not from the market generally.

Stakeholders. Persons with a stake in the operations of a company, whether by ownership, financial interest or otherwise.

Statement of changes in equity. A statement reporting on changes in SHAREHOLDERS' EQUITY during an accounting period. Changes include movements in retained earnings, items of income and expense recognized directly in equity, and movements in each class of share and each reserve.

Statement of recognized income and expense (SORIE). Statement showing all gains and losses for an accounting period, not just those passed through the INCOME STATEMENT. Does not include transactions with shareholders such as dividends.

Statements of recommended practice (SORPs). Non-mandatory statements of accounting practice, applicable to the financial statements of organizations such as charities and universities.

Statements of standard accounting practice (SSAPs). Under UK GAAP, statements prepared by the former Accounting Standards Committee. They are still applicable (other than to statements prepared under IFRS) to the extent that they have not been superseded by the FRS of the Accounting Standards Board.

Stock exchange. A market where shares, debentures, government securities, etc. are bought and sold.

Stocks. UK alternative term for INVENTORIES.

Stock turnover. *See* INVENTORY TURNOVER.

Straight-line depreciation. Method of depreciation in which the periodic charge is obtained by dividing the cost less residual value of the asset by its estimated economic life.

Subsidiary company. A company which is controlled by a parent company.

Substance over form. An accounting concept whereby transactions or other events are accounted for and presented in accordance with their economic substance rather than their legal form.

Summary financial statements. Financial statements summarizing the information contained in the annual report permitted to be sent to the shareholders of listed companies. They are not required to be sent to shareholders who do not request them.

Supplementary financial statements. Statements presented as additional to those required by law or other regulation.

Systematic (market) risk. Risk arising from the market, not from factors specific to a company. Quantified as the BETA of a company's ordinary shares.

Take-over bid. An offer to purchase all, or a controlling percentage of, the share capital of a company.

Tangible fixed assets. Alternative term for PROPERTY, PLANT AND EQUIPMENT and INVESTMENT PROPERTY.

Taxable income. Income liable to tax. Not usually equal to the profit before tax reported in a company's financial statements.

Tax credit. A credit received by shareholders at the same time as a dividend. Its amount is related to the rate of INCOME TAX. It can be set off against the liability to tax on the gross dividend.

Temporary differences. Differences between the tax basis of assets and liabilities and their reported amounts in the financial statements that will result in taxable or deductible amounts in future years when the reported amounts of the assets and liabilities are recovered or settled. *See* DEFERRED TAXATION.

Times interest earned. The number of times that a company's interest payable is covered or earned by its profit before interest and tax.

Trade credit. Short-term source of funds arising from credit granted by suppliers of goods.

Trading on the equity. Using fixed interest sources of capital to boost the return on the SHAREHOLDERS' EQUITY.

True and fair view. The overriding financial reporting requirement for companies under UK GAAP. The phrase is undefined but normally involves compliance with APPLICABLE ACCOUNTING STANDARDS. *A* true and fair view is required, not *the* true and fair view.

Turnover. Sales. Comprises amounts received from the provision of goods and services falling within a company's ordinary activities, after deduction of trade discounts, VAT and similar taxes. In consolidated financial statements it excludes inter-company transactions.

UK GAAP. The financial reporting rules applicable to UK companies which are not required or do not choose to follow INTERNATIONAL GAAP.

Undistributable reserves. The aggregate of share premium account; capital redemption reserve; accumulated unrealized profits, so far as not previously capitalized, less accumulated unrealized losses, so far as not previously written off in a reduction or reorganization of capital; and other reserves which a company is prohibited from distributing.

Unit trust. An undertaking formed to invest in securities (mainly ordinary shares) under the terms of a trust deed. Unlike an INVESTMENT TRUST it is not a company. The US equivalent is a mutual fund.

Unlimited company. A company the liability of whose members is limited neither by shares nor by guarantee.

Unsecured loan. Money borrowed by a company without the giving of security.

Valuation adjustment. An adjustment, such as DEPRECIATION or an allowance for DOUBTFUL DEBTS, that reduces the carrying value of an asset or liability.

Value added statement. A statement showing for an accounting period the wealth created (value added) by the operations of an enterprise and how the wealth has been distributed among employees, government, providers of capital, and replacement and expansion.

Value added tax (VAT). A tax based on the value added as goods pass from a supplier of raw materials, to a manufacturer, then to a wholesaler, then to a retailer, and finally to a consumer. Tax receivable can be set off against tax payable. Turnover is shown net of VAT in published income statements.

Value in use. The value discounted to the present of the estimated future net cash receipts from an asset.

Value relevance. The statistical association between the disclosure of an item in a company's financial statements and movements in its share price.

Warrants. Certificates giving a right to holders to purchase a security at a predetermined price at a future date or dates.

Window-dressing. The manipulation of figures in financial statements (especially current assets and current liabilities) so as to produce a desired appearance and ratios on the balance sheet date.

Working capital. Current assets net of current liabilities.

Work in progress. Partly completed manufactured goods.

Writing-down allowance. The annual amount deductible for tax purposes on certain tangible fixed assets.

Written-down value. The value of an asset in a company's accounting records or for tax purposes after depreciation or capital allowances have been deducted.

Yield. The rate of return relating cash invested to cash received or expected to be received.

Z-score. A measure of the SOLVENCY of a company calculated from an equation incorporating more than one financial ratio.

Index